The Environment and Cosmic Metabolism:

Looking at the stars and thinking about the Earth

A very personal tribute to Wilhelm Reich

By Peter Ind
April 2007

Bargepole Publishing Limited

P.O. Box 403
Twickenham
U.K.

Published by Bargepole Publishing Limited

© Peter Ind 1964, 1979 and 2007

All rights reserved. No part of this publication may be reproduced or transmitted in any form or by any means, electronic or mechanical, including photocopying, recording or any information, storage or retrieval system, without prior permission in writing from the publishers.

ISBN 978-0-9558062-0-9 (Paperback)

Design and typesetting by Nils Solberg
nils@nilssolberg.com
Cover images courtesy of NASA
Printed and bound in Great Britain by Antony Rowe,
Chippenham, Wiltshire

www.jazzcorner.com (see bass players - Peter Ind)
waveindjones@aol.com

This book is dedicated to the memory of Wilhelm Reich (26th March 1897 – 3rd November 1957) in his fiftieth anniversary year (2007)

I would also like to acknowledge the Wilhelm Reich Foundation for keeping that memory alive and for ensuring that the body of his work is preserved.

ACKNOWLEDGEMENTS

Firstly, I want to express my gratitude to my partner Dr. Susan Jones who has been of immense help in advising and editing. It has made what is an extremely difficult and new concept easily readable. After writing the original Cosmic Metabolism and Vortical Accretion in 1964 the task of explaining those concepts simply has been most difficult. It is thanks to Sue's tireless help that I can now present it as the first accessible thesis.

I am also thankful for my late friend musician Jeff Morton who introduced me to Wilhelm Reich's writings. I cannot picture what the course of my life would have been had I not discovered the profound truths that lay in Reich's written work. Developing this knowledge and becoming aware of what I have come to describe as Cosmic Metabolism has been very lonely and frustrating. I owe much to one friend in particular Salo Boekbinder, who affirmed in his own inimitable way the validity of what I have been writing. To the late Lennie Tristano my musical mentor, with whom I spent many memorable hours discussing Reich's work and the conviction we both held of the supremacy of his discoveries, many thanks. I also need to give due credit to the artist, the late Wayne Nowack, for his constant interest and support for my work over the years. Most recently there has been the much appreciated enthusiastic support of Kevin Hinchey of the Wilhelm Reich Institute in Rangeley, Maine, USA. after he received a pre publication draft of this book.

I now launch it on the stormy seas of today's world, hoping that someone will uncork this bottle and treasure the message within.

PREFACE

Twenty or even ten years ago if anyone had seriously warned about climate change the general reaction would have been dismissive. Today it has become clear that the world is now faced with a global crisis that appears insurmountable unless we drastically reduce the amount of pollutants we are creating. The core of the problem lays in our total dependency upon energy obtained from fossil fuels. Debates on how to resolve this crisis centre upon how to lessen the pollution we are creating and how to develop alternative energy systems that are non-pollutive. The concepts aired so far, though valuable, do little more than to try to alleviate the problem of pollution. Our dependency upon fossil fuels for energy (particularly portable forms of energy) cannot be resolved as long as we view energy as needing to be sourced from the breakdown of matter – whether coal, oil or natural gas – or even nuclear fission.

A second and equally crucial aspect of the dilemma we find ourselves in is the inescapable fact that fossil fuels will not last forever and already these are becoming harder to access. Thus there is a kind of fatalistic aspect to all these discussions. The unspoken fear is that we are living in a time when the concept of an ideal of "affluence for all" may never be possible.

My outlook is very different. For the major part of my life I have learned that there is a way forward, an understanding that, although already a part of human knowledge, has nevertheless been mainly ignored or demeaned.

It is the reality of a fundamental cosmic energy manifesting in a variety of ways – and humanity has failed to come to grips with this. The way forward lies in the recognition of this power. This sounds messianic. It is not; just common sense if you are prepared to accept the evidence. The changes to come will be based on the acceptance of this prime reality. When eventually this becomes common knowledge it will lead to the further development of a science that the majority of present day scientists are unaware of. My thesis embraces the work of two major scientists of the twentieth century, mainly Wilhelm Reich but also Nicola Tesla. Reich was persecuted for his research and Tesla's research was used in part without full recognition and much of his most important work remains unappreciated and unused. My aim is to dislodge outdated concepts and make room for a deeper perspective of reality than now prevails.

Fire energy was the energy of the caveman. It is time to move forward.

Peter Ind
Auvers-sur-Oise
November 2007

Comment from Dr. Simeon Tropp's son, Bill

I can still remember so vividly my father's excitement when he came to know Peter Ind in the 1960s. My father had worked closely with Wilhelm Reich during his years in America (1939-1957) and had been his chief financial supporter, as well as his student, patient, colleague and friend. Reich's close associates were primarily MD psychoanalysts; my father had obtained degrees in chemistry and physics before moving to medicine and was thus better equipped to understand the direction Reich was moving in during this last period.

By the 1960s, just a few years after Reich's tragic death in prison, Reich's circle was immured in pessimism, nostalgia, resentment, lassitude, and in-fighting. The light had gone. Nobody was doing anything! The revolutionaries were reverting to the petit bourgeois types from which most had sprung. It was sad and it was outrageous.

Now came Peter Ind, a kind of Blakeian figure reluctantly thrown up by the English once a generation or so. A brilliant musician as well as a brilliant scientist, his experience of Reich was not coloured by personal encounters with Reich; he was neither blessed nor cursed (one thinks of Reich's disastrous relationship with Einstein) in that special way. He was one of the very few my father ever met who was capable of understanding Reich's thought without becoming overwhelmed by it. And he was making original contributions of his own at a time when everyone in Reich's own circle had lost the will to originate thought.

This was a colossal gift for my father in his last years. Here was someone who could be relied upon to further thought in a way that even Reich would have approved.

My father had served America in the Great War; he had some reckless heroic moments in the Second World War; he had lived through the United States government's senseless persecution of Reich. He had, in other words, much personal experience of tragedy and horror, and no sensible reason to believe the world might change. Yet he retained always a kind of warmth and wisdom which I see echoed in Peter Ind. But echo is not quite the right word, for Peter, though open to influence, has always sung his own tune, just as Reich did before him. Above all this, perhaps, is what my father recognised in him. It gave him much delight, as this new book, so much more accessible than its predecessors, will delight those to come.

CONTENTS

Acknowledgements — iv
Preface — v
Comment from Dr. Simeon Tropp's son, Bill — vi

Introduction – What on Earth is Cosmic Metabolism? — 1
The renewal of energy

Introducing a Different Conception of Energy — 5
Looking at the stars

Section 1 – Wilhelm Reich and the Science of the Far Future
An understanding of cosmic energy

Chapter 1. Reich's Influence on My Life: — 14
Keeping an Open Mind
Chapter 2. The Conclusions I came to about Reich's — 19
Findings on Energy:
The Cosmos is not 'out there', but linked to us
Chapter 3. Developing Ideas, Building Understanding: — 28
The difficulty of explaining new concepts

Section 2 – Extract from 1964 Writing:
Cosmic Metabolism and Vortical Accretion
Open and enthusiastic

Chapter 4 – Cosmic Metabolism and Vortical Accretion: — 39
Understanding cosmic energy

Section 3 – Extract from 1979 Writing:
Cosmic Metabolism and Cosmic Energy
Feeling like a lone voice

Chapter 5 - Cosmic Metabolism and Cosmic Energy: — 56
Dissipative as well as Expansive Properties of Energy

Section 4 – Not Just the Carbon Footprint
but Crucially the Radiation Footprint
Older, wiser and hopeful

Chapter 6 – Science is tied up in packages: — 66
The energy potential we ignore and why
Chapter 7 – Reflecting again on Reich in 2007: — 75
Thinking about the Earth

Bibliography
Some initial references — 85

CONTENTS

Acknowledgements
Preface
Comment from Dr. Simeon Tropp's son, Bill

Introduction – What on Earth is Cosmic Metabolism?
The renewal of energy

Introducing a Different Conception of Energy
Looking at the stars

Section 1 – Wilhelm Reich and the Science of the far future
An understanding of cosmic energy

Chapter 1. Reich's influence on my life.
Keeping an Open Mind
Chapter 2. The Experiments Einstein rejected; Reich's radical new Energy.
The Cosmos is not 'no-thing', but linked to us.
Chapter 3. Developing ideas, Building Understanding.
The difficulty of applying a new concepts

Section 2 – Extract from 1964 writing.
Cosmic Metabolism and Vernon Ney (Our great and enthusiastic...

Chapter 4 – On my 15th journey into cosmic Metabolism
Understanding cosmic energy.

Section 3 – Extract from 1979 Writing
Cosmic Metabolism and Cosmic Energy
Feeling like a lone voice

Chapter 5. Cosmic Metabolism and Cosmic Energy;
Dissipative as well as Expansive Properties of Energy

Section 4 – Not Just the Carbon footprint
But Crucially, the Radiation footprint.
Water, water and health

Chapter 6. Science is tied up in paradigms
The energy potential we ignore and why
Chapter 7. Balancing Spam on Earth in 2017
Thinking about the Earth

Bibliography
Some initial references

Introduction - What on Earth is Cosmic Metabolism?

The renewal of energy

It is a question that people have often asked me when I talk about energy and cosmic metabolism. Really simply, Cosmic Metabolism is the process of energy renewal. What happens in the cosmos is crucial to Earth and our environment. I wanted, in this 50th anniversary year after Reich's death, to write a short introduction about this process of energy renewal for people who are concerned about the environment and not clear what to do about it but also not convinced that current theorists have got the answer either!

Wilhelm Reich's scientific work even today is still important to a consideration of cosmic energy and the current debates about pollution and the environment. Reich's work led me to an understanding about energy renewal and Cosmic Metabolism, which I know is so important to the health of our own planet but which means thinking about energy in a different way. I decided that the best way to help readers to understand this is to show how my ideas developed over time; this is therefore a very personal account of my experiences of Reich.

In this foreword I will start with an introduction to Cosmic Metabolism. There are two ideas here - cosmic and metabolism. Beginning with a consideration of the cosmos, I can illustrate this quite simply:

Every day the earth revolves on its axis and never returns to the same place - NEVER - yet we still cling to the delusion that the sun rises and sets each day. This is a myth. In fact the cosmos, within which the Earth is embedded with the Sun, the Moon, the other planets, all the stars and galaxies, is in continual movement. This is an essential aspect to the health of our planet. We need to look at the stars and think about Earth.

I will explore some of these myths about the cosmos and draw some different conclusions about cosmic energy and what this means for all our debates about the environment and pollution. But to talk about the cosmos and Cosmic Metabolism immediately raises suspicions. Unless you are a scientist with a reputation, to discuss this seems somehow pretentious, egotistical or plain crazy. Even the phrase 'head in the clouds' or 'on another planet' suggest you don't have a sense of reality. But what could be more real than thinking about the power that turns the world?

That is what is happening all around you in the cosmos. In the ten minutes it will take you to read this foreword, the earth including us, will have moved 10 minutes of arc in its daily rotation, or the equivalent of 160 miles along the Equator. It has also moved in its annual trajectory, or journey around the Sun almost 11,000 miles in that time. Added to this during the same period, the Sun (including the whole solar system) will have moved 7,000 miles towards the constellation of Lyra, close to the star Vega[1]. None of us, the Earth, the Sun or any other planets in the cosmos will return to the same position - EVER.

Maybe this will strike you as astounding or frightening. It could be too frightening to even want to think further. But the truth is that the cosmos, the sun, the planets, the stars and the galaxies are all in a constant state of flux. That is what has always fascinated me.

But here is another myth perpetuated in our culture. All of this incredible complex movement is said to be something that was set in motion, rather like the movements of a clock, at "the beginning of time" and present day cosmic movement is resultant from some presumed upheaval "at the beginning". However, it has long been realised, in the scientific world, that the motion of the earth is not steady. The length of the day varies, the length of the year varies and there have been annual variations in the past. All these facts undermine the idea that cosmic movement is set and solidly established from this supposed primal event. Intermittently the earth slows down and speeds up. Like the myth of the sun rising and setting, orthodox astronomy knows these facts but does not focus on them as significant.

However, for the Earth to retain its annual movement in spite of fluctuations is an aspect of the huge and powerful force, the cosmic energy that keeps it all revolving. And it is cosmic energy that underlines this movement and can be tapped as a source of energy. This is entirely different from the expansive energy we produce from combustion, whether it be from oil, coal, "green" fuels or even that most deadly of expansive energies - nuclear power. We currently think of energy in this very narrow way.

In a way we do tap into the cosmic energy - but in a particular way. We generate electricity but we do not see it as part of a broader concept of energy. Instead there is the myth that electricity is the mere movement of electrons within circuitry. But we need to understand that electricity is one aspect of cosmic force or energy. The generation of electricity draws on some of this energy from the cosmos - from space.

Which brings me to the second concept - metabolism. What does this have to do with this cosmic process I have just described? Again, in simple terms, metabolism is the reality of change. It is what happens when one thing becomes something else. To use an everyday example; we take in food which is from other organic material. We obtain energy from the food. We metabolise the food into energy. We excrete what we do not need and it then, as fertiliser, becomes part of another cycle of metabolism in the growth of food.

It is easy to understand metabolism in terms of the food chain. We use this analogy in other specific processes. But metabolism is happening on a continuous basis, not just for us or in our food chain; but it is essentially a cosmic process. This has not yet gained acceptance. Space is not an empty void. (Just think about it - why is there such a vastness without any

---

[1] Extrapolated from the Larousse Encyclopaedia of Astronomy

purpose?) Space has the function of cleaning waste energy; ultimately it is the way energy is renewed and replenished. Cosmic Metabolism is the name I chose for this process of energy renewal.

But with current pollution levels so high, we are putting too much into the atmosphere, more than it can handle and the metabolic balance of the Earth is severely upset. Cosmic Metabolism is, as I said at the beginning, crucial to the Earth and our environment. And it is this balance that we have lost.

Cosmic energy is what we need to focus on. This is what Reich learned to understand and demonstrated in his experiments. Reich's work leads us to a practical understanding of universal energy functions that are within us, underlie all life and extend throughout the cosmos. Reich was not the only one. Nikola Tesla also needs to be mentioned here. He was the scientist who gave us AC electricity; he understood this principle of cosmic energy. He may never have directly stated it but his writings indicate his comprehension of this and it is reflected in his discoveries. Conceptualising cosmic energy is not new but the puzzle is that this energy source is consistently ignored. Why? That is the question I will answer, with acknowledgement particularly to Reich in this essay.

Perhaps this essay should come with a psychic health warning. If you cannot be open to the ideas above then maybe read no further!

If you want to take that step, this essay is organised to provide you with some different perspectives. Firstly the Introduction sets out a different perspective on energy. Then Section 1 provides background information of how I was introduced to Reich (Chapter 1), how I studied and undertook some of his experiments that changed how I viewed energy (Chapter 2) and how I then tried to interest others in the concept of cosmic energy that Reich realised is the energy of life (Chapter 3).

Having, hopefully, made some of the concepts and Reich's ideas more understandable, I will share some technical considerations I have made during more than forty years of studying and searching. Section 2 provides you with more technical discussion about Cosmic Metabolism and cosmic energy. In this second section Chapter 4 is an excerpt from the book I printed in Big Sur, California (September 1964) entitled Cosmic Metabolism and Vortical Accretion. Section 3 is also a more technical discussion but from a synopsis written in 1979. The extract, in Chapter 5, provides further reflection on expansive and contractive energy and how this sits with the world of astronomy and science, after a further 13-year consideration.

The final section, Section 4, provides a conclusion. I think that, by this stage, you too will be asking why is there such a blind spot about a consideration of Reich's work and the concept of cosmic energy? So this final section provides a further reflection, in 2007, about Cosmic Metabolism and the environment. In this section, Chapter 6 is a reconsideration of the reaction of the scientific community to Reich's work, their response to my own consideration of his work and why they are so dismissive of Reich. In the final chapter, Chapter 7, my concern is to look afresh and with an open mind at the cosmos, Cosmic Metabolism, cosmic energy and our crucial need to take Reich's work seriously in our deliberations about pollution, climate change, fossil fuel, the environment and our future.

There is so much more to say in detail about Reich and his work and I will include this discussion in the book I am currently finalising. This essay is intended as an introduction for those who might be inspired, in this anniversary year, to want to know some more about him. I have not included a detailed list of references, but a list of some initial books that you might want to look at is provided at the end of this essay.

If you are interested enough to read this essay, you are as deeply concerned about the environment and our planet as I am. But be warned! I have shown in Chapters 3 and 6 the difficulties and responses I have had over the last 40 years to these ideas. You might find the same negativity. We all want to help but we rely on others, with expertise, to show us what to do. But we also need to have the best understanding so we know that what others propose as the way to improve our environment are truly effective rather than being politically, egotistically or financially motivated. And shame on those politicians who currently and cynically use our concern about the environment as a means to raise taxes.

In contrast, Reich has provided me with such inspiration. I hope this essay will give you the enthusiasm to at least go and look at some of his writing - Reich wrote so clearly and easily and his work is even more relevant after 50 years. It gives a new direction for how we could cope with our increasing energy needs without crippling the planet.

Introducing a Different Conception of Energy

Looking at the stars

"The eye only sees what the mind is prepared to comprehend"
Henri Bergson

This essay centres around the concept of energy and what this means in terms of our present day culture. In a way we take it for granted but when we look around us, when we look up into the sky, if we ever peer out to space we are looking at energy, but do we understand it?

The reason why we need to understand energy now

Our current sources of energy lie mainly in the use of fossil fuels. These are not inexhaustible and there is great concern as to how long such fuels will last, with the additional concern of what will replace them as a sustainable energy source.

The effect of relying on fossil fuels has resulted in massive atmospheric and environmental pollution. This has already upset the ecological balance and resulted in what we have come to describe as 'global warming'. Though the ecological disturbances are not entirely caused by the massive use of fossil fuels to obtain energy, it is believed that a major cause of these disturbances is due to energy obtained in this way. There is no agreement about the various alternate energy sources as a viable substitute for what we are currently using. But it is not surprising that there is much uncertainty as to how long we can sustain our present course of energy usage.

Before we can gain a clear overview of the present dilemma as regards energy it is essential to consider why energy seemingly has to be accessed in the way it is, primarily using the expansive aspect of fire.

Historically energy through steam power

Let us briefly take a look at history. Prior to the invention of steam power and the development of the steam engine, energy was mainly provided by the muscular power of men and animals. There was also wind power (windmills and sailing ships for example) plus a limited amount of power provided by watermills. Thus atmospheric pollution was limited to such activities as the smelting of metals and the manufacture of ceramics in the days before steam.

When mankind discovered the latent power in steam the giant leap to what we now regard as the industrial revolution began. It led eventually to mass production and to the beginning of the emancipation of travel. Soon railways became mass transport - for people and goods. Locomotives fired by wood or coal became a feature of civilisation and such transport spread world-wide. Steam power became the feature of the nineteenth century. All of this had an effect on the atmosphere and increased the levels of pollution people faced.

Even in the late eighteenth century when steam power and the industrial revolution that followed noticeably affected the atmosphere, this was largely confined to industrial districts with open countryside affected little if at all. This situation prevailed even as late as the nineteen thirties. Such pollution seldom spread beyond the areas where it was generated. It is only since World War Two that pollution became as pervasive as we now know it.

The internal combustion engine

By the end of the nineteenth century, a new form of motive power began to be developed. This was the internal combustion engine - power that depended on oil - either petroleum or diesel fuel. Both steam power and power from the internal combustion engine ran side by side although gradually the internal combustion engine became far more widespread. Now in the twenty first century various forms of internal combustion, such as diesel, petrol engines, jets and rockets dominate almost to the exclusion of steam power. Thanks to oil and its fuel derivatives the twentieth century also became the century of flight. In theory this situation could last far into the future were it not for the fact that oil is becoming harder to access, and there are justifiable fears that the oil culture will inevitably come to a close at some future date.

Opinions about when this will occur vary considerably. It will depend partly on efforts to further develop renewable energy sources, though currently there is little indication that these could totally replace the oil culture. At best they would only be of limited help to reduce fossil fuel consumption.

Expansive fire energy

We have become dependent on the world of technology and it is now difficult to conceive of the world being any different. This culture of technology was made possible by exploiting the energy of fire. Why fire? Fire is expansive and it is the harnessing of the expansive energy of fire that has given us the power that underlies technological development. I can hear you questioning that assertion. What about electricity you may ask. Yes that is so, but we need power to drive the generators that provide us with electricity. This can be provided by water turbines, as in hydroelectric installations. In that case the energy to drive the turbines comes from the gravitational potential of falling water. However to generate electrical power we need an energy source to overcome the magnetic torque created in the generator. It is well known that all the wind and water powered electrical generating stations cannot provide sufficient electrical energy to replace that provided by steam turbines, and these derive their energy from fire.

It is therefore essential to realise that our use of energy, whether for transport i.e. automobiles; aircraft and ships or any of the myriad other uses for which coal or oil provide the motive power, means that energy is primarily from fossil fuels and the energy of fire.

Nuclear energy

When in 1945 the energy from the atomic nucleus was first released, the energy generated was of such magnitude it led to the misconception that this was truly the cosmic energy. This was viewed as the fundamental energy of the stars. The power of nuclear energy dwarfs that of energy obtained from chemical breakdown, such as the burning of oil products or of other fossil fuels.

But it is a mistake to conclude that nuclear energy is the prime cosmic energy, simply because of the magnitude of the energy released through atomic fission. This has led in turn to the belief that the entire cosmos is expanding from a primeval super nuclear beginning known familiarly as the 'Big Bang'. I view it differently and discuss this in detail in Sections 3 and 4. As an introduction, for our current consideration of energy here, nuclear and fire energy both need to be seen as expansive forms of energy.

Cosmic energy - the other aspect of energy

Fire energy - through fossil fuels and nuclear fission, is in fact just one aspect of a cosmic duality. It is the expansive, dispersive aspect. The other is the energy of material formation; it is the spiral cosmic energy - the vortex, the energy that powers the turning of the earth, the sun and cosmic bodies. It is also as Wilhelm Reich discovered - the energy of life. To ascribe vortical energy as merely being the churning of the aftermath of a presumed 'Big Bang' is a gigantic error and part of the myth that cosmic energy is solely the energy of fire.

Cosmic Metabolism

I discussed in the foreword how we ignore this cosmic energy and how we also ignore how the universe, space, the cosmos, renews waste energy by allowing it to expand and it is this that transforms it into fresh cosmic energy. We do already draw down this source of energy, though unaware that this is what takes place when we generate electricity

How does this happen? Quite simply the energy contracts as it is pulled down into the magnetic field, a vortex that condenses it. Having drawn in the cosmic energy, our electrical devices then use it - now in the form of electricity - and in performing work it is then dispersed as radiation. It is not merely a matter of electrons flowing through a circuit. Electrical generators create a magnetic vortex. You can visualise it as a similar process as the spiral of water going down the plughole. This vortex impels the cosmic energy into metallic matter - the energy then becomes what we recognise as electricity. Having performed the work of operating our electrical devices it is then released as radiation - the dissipative aspect of electricity.

Realisation is dawning that the biggest problem of our present day culture is that of pollution, much of it from fossil fuels, but also, less acknowledged, from radiation. When we burn fossil fuel we produce heat energy (expansive energy) and this is dispersed. Whenever matter breaks down, whether as fuel to power our engines or for energy in the form of food, it dissipates back into the atmosphere and ultimately to the outer cosmos. Dissipation takes place in very different ways. It happens on the chemical level, that we term "pollution". Radiation is also dissipation. We understand this in a very practical way - great distances are needed before radiation signals such as TV transmission become totally dispersed and lost in the radiation background.

The orthodox view is that once we extract energy from fossil fuel and use it to power our machines it is just waste. That is because we only see energy as being an expansive process. It is not that it just breaks down and down into nothing. We can see from the example of the food chain and ourselves that that is not right. Dissipation of stale used energy - something that we disregard as being ultimately mere waste, is an essential aspect of Cosmic Metabolism. It is the beginning of the cleansing process and, in fact, a way of renewing used energy into life giving energy. To appreciate this reality thoroughly we have to divest our minds of all the accepted "explanations" - that are not so much wrong in themselves but are viewed as isolated concepts - preventing us from understanding the totality and unity underlying cosmic functions.

This process of both contraction and expansion is part of the cosmic energy flow; it is an example of Cosmic Metabolism here on Earth. Whereas fire energy is expansive, dissipative, and dispersive - the energy of the vortex is condensative, formative and creative, it is the counterpart of the cosmic duality. It is essential to comprehend these facts before reading further. Both aspects of expansion (fire) and contraction (the Vortex) are interwoven - realising this will pave the way out of our current energy dilemma.

Our energy crisis and people's fear

Western efforts to control oil supplies have been considerably eroded during the past half-century. When Mossadeq took control of Iran, this resulted in the demise of the Anglo-Iranian Oil Company, through the nationalisation of Iranian oil. The British politicians reacted indignantly as though the Iranians had no right to the oil found in their territory. At the time most British politicians regarded Iran and other Middle Eastern territories as "protectorates" and accused them of breaking the agreements over oil. This they certainly did but today such kinds of agreement would be seen as totally one sided and manifestly unfair - a relic of a colonial past in which Europeans and Americans were able to dominate world politics and trade.

Since World War Two there has been a gradual erosion of the power wielded by Europe. America became and remained the prime super power, with Communist Russia becoming regarded as a second super power. Power playing and stopping other emerging competitors continues. The development of nuclear fission, brought a new fear into the world, primarily over the awesome and deathly reality of atomic weapons, and secondly of the fear that such technical know-how might become common knowledge. This fear at first embedded in conscious awareness, has become less obvious, as new generations came into being that never knew a world free from the nuclear threat. But the fear is now embedded in our plasm. Additionally what we loosely refer to as "the West" is becoming fearful of losing its position of apparent supremacy and the resentment that has built up over the West's material wealth poses another threat as the power of the West is eroded still further. Though the Russian super power dissolved into a group of individual states and the so-called 'cold war' fears receded, other anxieties became apparent. The 9/11 attack that destroyed New York's trade towers brought to the fore another aspect of power; of those who traded their lives in attempts to bring America (and by association the West) to its knees.

Just as over a half century earlier one fanatic - Adolf Hitler - came near to world domination, so another group of fanatics have succeeded in instilling a fear amongst Western societies, that the West's dominance and prosperity is beginning to be seriously threatened. The current oil crisis has emerged through several factors. First those countries that are sources of oil are emerging as power centres in their own right (OPEC) etc, and secondly the old colonial tactic of divide and rule is turning against the West - especially with the proliferation of arms. The general fears over proliferation of nuclear weapons include the fear of terrorists obtaining and using such weapons. In short we now live in a culture of apprehension.

The future and fossil fuels

At the forefront of this fear is the certainty that oil is a finite resource and will not last forever. Unlike most mineral resources that can be recycled, oil, apart from its use in the manufacture of plastics, disappears in smoke and pollution.

There is one seemingly inevitable thread that runs throughout human history. That is the greed for power. Whether or not we believe the desire for power to be natural or a perversion of the life within us, it has always persisted and ruled human life. Not everyone is dominated by such desire, but the need to dominate motivates so many and there seems little likelihood that humanity will ever be any different in that respect. At the moment everyone is trying to climb on board the green bandwagon not least the politicians who see a golden opportunity for "green taxes".

To me it appears criminal to continue to plunder the planet for oil and coal – merely to burn these valuable resources. Developing the latent power of cosmic energy will bring about a very different human world – as remote from today's society, as we are from the ancient Greeks.

Though humanity has not succeeded in overcoming strife, does that mean that we should resign ourselves to this fact and continue to sit on our hands? In the two hundred plus years since we became emancipated from muscle power, huge achievements have taken place. Even if some espouse a view that we would be better off without the technology that we have developed, we cannot go back. The dream of rural peace, of life without the "satanic mills", is an illusion.

As humans we only have ourselves to blame. Of course the discovery of steam power revolutionised the world. Steam power was overtaken by the development of the internal combustion engine and led to an emancipation of transport including of course air travel. The steam train, the marvel of my childhood, is now only a tourist curiosity.

The eventual exhaustion of fossil fuels is something that few want to face. Currently proposed alternatives come with a sense of restricted activity. The kind of freedom of movement of today cannot be maintained should we be forced to fall back on the alternatives as conceived. The future looks bleak if you accept this view. But we have another option. It became clear to me through years of study and consideration of what others have written (and facing rejection of my views too!)

Can this be true?

Surely there cannot be another approach to the energy crisis – I hear you say. The sceptics among you will almost certainly be muttering that surely someone would have come forward before now if it was true? Can I be saying that there is a way forward with this idea, that doesn't just mean amalgamating a series of "green" alternatives? YES that is what I am saying.

Two very different scientists knew of this energy potential. They became aware of it from totally different standpoints. The first, Nikola Tesla revolutionised our knowledge and use of electricity, but a number of his ideas including a craft that defies gravity were never developed due to lack of funding. Wilhelm Reich discovered this energy potential that he called Orgone, through a systematic investigation of life and what Henri Bergson referred to as the "élan vitale". The problem remains simply that of a closed culture that is unable or unwilling to realise the potential of the cosmic energy; so blinkered that it only sees energy as the power of fire.

Tesla remained virtually unknown throughout his life, despite the worldwide use of his discoveries. Only very recently has this omission been rectified with Tesla now rated as one of the top hundred Americans. Reich had a very harsh fate – his discoveries were not just ignored but demeaned as fraudulent by the US Food and Drug Administration. He was jailed for alleged contempt of court – dying in jail whilst serving his sentence.

Upon what authority do I base these assertions of an entirely different energy source? When I was first introduced to Wilhelm Reich's writings I realised that here were concepts that reached way beyond the culture in which we are all immersed. In the nineteen fifties his work gave a vision of hope, of a world to come, of a world where humanity could begin to live in harmony - an inner harmony that develops from self-awareness overcoming the effects of sexual repression and not from climbing the ladder of commercial success. Sadly Reich's ideas were derailed. His ideas became a movement – the Sexual Revolution, the hippy movement that foundered because most hippies wanted an easy life, unwilling to put in the hard work both mentally and physically to achieve a better life. In California this was particularly appealing, with its comfortable climate and affluent lifestyles.

Though Reich inspired many, few stopped to realise the depth of his research and understanding. He knew what it was like to face both fascism and communism. He had experienced first hand the trauma's of World War One and the human misery in the years following. Paradoxically the USA the bastion of Capitalism came closer to what he termed "Work Democracy" than any of the attempted socialism reforms in War Weary Europe. Become orgastically potent and you too can become Superman – or Super stud – thus the powerful insights developed by Reich and his research, became demeaned by the dreamy visions of the hippy generation. That hippy way of life flowered just briefly – only too often degenerating into commune squalor. In the nineteen seventies I visited Christiana in Copenhagen and I found it frightening like a foreboding of a future lost society.

Nikola Tesla had that openness to the possibilities of what could be created. He knew he could build a craft that would become gravity free. All his inventions worked – and he is only now belatedly recognised, some sixty years after his death, as one of the all time great Americans. Of course his inventions needed financial backing. He did receive considerable backing for certain of his inventions – these were concepts that the financiers of his time could see profits to be made. But the concept of a gravity-defying vehicle was clearly beyond the vision of businessmen of his time. Tesla clearly realised aircraft fuelled by combustion were wasteful, dangerous and unnecessary. Wilhelm Reich understood the reality of cosmic energy – this simply from investigating living plasm. Both men approached this reality from differing viewpoints but through their researches they both became aware of the underlying cosmic energy.

We, or our descendants face the inevitability of scarcity of fossil fuels. Developing energy resources from the basic cosmic energy will allow us to use oil as a valuable material – and not to continually pollute – simply to produce the largely unnecessary fire energy. The problem is not so much how we find the way to harness the cosmic energy, but why we have ignored those who have pointed the way. Why was Tesla's insight ignored, though other discoveries of his have transformed the world? Why also was the peaceful scientist Reich pilloried and jailed – simply because his discoveries were demeaned and wrongly considered fraudulent? (And why is it that those who have realised this reality have been ignored or even persecuted?)

I have at times written about this but it often seems too much to accept. So for this essay I want to show you how my ideas developed and formed over a 40-year period and why I am now passionately convinced that the way forward is to face the reality of cosmic energy and take Cosmic Metabolism seriously.

Section 1

Wilhelm Reich and the Science of the Far Future

An understanding of Cosmic Energy

Chapter 1. Reich's Influence on My Life:

Keeping an open mind

"Imagination is more important than knowledge. For knowledge is limited to all we know and understand while imagination embraces the entire world, and all there ever will be to know and understand."

Albert Einstein

If I say there is a different way to look at the cosmos, cosmic energy and how we conceptualise space that is where the problem begins. People become dismissive or lose interest. It has happened many times. Why should this be?

After many years of contemplating this, I know that looking at the concept of cosmic or life energy requires a willingness to approach things differently and to be open to seeing what there is rather than just what we may have been taught. It means willingness to challenge opinions. All of that can be very difficult.

At times we are more open to new ideas and different ways of thinking, generally whilst we are still young. That is what happened to me. I was in my twenties, in New York and part of the jazz scene when it was at its height, playing with some of the most accomplished musicians. By the late 1950s I was living in a loft, recording music, painting and playing. I was introduced to Reich's writings and the descriptions of his experiments and this it is where this journey begins.

How I was affected by Reich's work

Reich and his work wove through my life at the time. I have written about this recently, in the book about Lennie Tristano, the blind New York jazz pianist. Lennie recommended that I read the writings of both Freud and Reich. I regard them as the main pioneers of psychological insights in the twentieth century. The jazz drummer, Jeff Morton, lent me one of Reich's books - "The Function of the Orgasm". Many musicians and artists in that 1950's New York loft scene were interested in psychology and read Reich as much as Jung and Freud[2] - such as Dave Lambert of the Lambert, Hendricks and Ross vocal group. We discussed Reich's work at length; Dave visited my loft specifically because he knew of my interest in Reich. The famous expressionist artist De Kooning was also involved with Reich's concepts and spent time in therapy with Dr. Simeon Tropp, one of the doctors trained by Reich. Adam Margoshes the correspondent for the New York Village Voice who wrote the Obituary article about Reich also wrote an Introduction for my 1964 work Cosmic Metabolism and Vortical Accretion. Later while living in California I met the politician, Adlai Stevenson's[3] mother-in-law who told me Adlai had all of Reich's writings.

---

[2] Although Jung was seen as a key influence in psychological thinking at the time, he was less appealing to me. For me the core of both Freud's and Reich's work was the concept of energy.

[3] Adlai Stevenson had been a presidential candidate in the US, who allegedly lost because he was divorced.

I mention these names only to illustrate that there were people from various walks of life at that time that followed his work.

Reich's work was particularly well known to many in the jazz community. I had some in-depth discussions with Lennie Tristano about Reich's work. He was profoundly influenced by Reich. I spent some time reading to Lennie from Reich's books, since they were unavailable as talking books. Lennie offered to play a free concert at Reich's Institute in Maine. However, by that time, although we didn't know it, they were being harassed by the US Food and Drug Administration (FDA) Inspectors. This was during the height of the crucial Oranur experimentation, which I will discuss later in Chapter 7. We were unaware then of the difficulties they faced and our projected concert never happened.

Even Charlie Parker the incredible saxophonist, known to jazz musicians as Bird, talked to me about Reich. He said he believed Reich was correct in everything he had written though Bird felt it was too late for him personally to benefit from Reichian therapy as other jazz musicians had done. Sadly he died at 34 years of age. He had also told pianist Ronnie Ball that he read Reich's books during the time he spent at Camarillo State Hospital, where he went following a breakdown while playing in Los Angeles. Reich's books were generally available in those days. You could buy them in bookshops in New York and other major US cities.

My shock at the way Reich was treated

Reich was internationally well known and respected. He taught at New York's New School of Social Research in the late 1940's. It came therefore as a shock to discover that the US Food and Drug Administration were formulating a case against him for alleged fraudulent practice. This eventually undermined his work and finally led to his being jailed and his untimely death in jail. I still have a copy of the injunction against Reich; we were all so concerned (and initially disbelieving) about what was happening that we obtained copies. It seemed a terrible mistake and miscarriage of justice.

When the injunction came out I visited the FDA offices in Manhattan to protest; I was alone and, when they began to question me about my motives and my status as an immigrant, I realised that these people meant business. It was frightening. It was the first time in my life that I had come across the negative power of the State. It became clear that the FDA regarded Reich as guilty even before the trial.

I kept all the newspaper articles that I could find about what was happening, including the burning of his books in the Gannsevoort Incinerator in downtown Manhattan. I must include a comment here by Sigmund Freud, which I think sums up such action:

"What progress we are making. In the Middle Ages they would have burned me. Now they are content with burning my books."

I did not go to Reich's trial in Maine as I was playing in New York, but I had friends who went and reported back on how the first judge appeared sympathetic to Reich then the trial was adjourned and the judge was replaced by someone else. They didn't know why. They told me that the prosecuting counsel, trying to find something against Reich, had to descend to the level of querying how he paid his cigarette bill. Both Reich and his co-worker Dr. Michael Silvert MD were jailed on charges of alleged contempt of court and, at the time of sentencing, the New York Times made the remarkable printers error of describing Reich as Dr. Reign of the Wilhelm Reich Institute - causing people to wonder "Surely this could not be the famous psychologist Reich?"

Dr. Silvert was sentenced to one year in prison and Reich to two years, but Reich was due for parole after a year. However he died two weeks before parole, reportedly from heart failure. Sadly his colleague Dr Silvert allegedly committed suicide after his release.

At the time of Reich's death in the Lewisburg, Pennsylvania Penitentiary I was on a plane flying to Syracuse, having taken a part time job as an estimator for a building construction company (money was tight at the time). The cabin crew handed out copies of the New York Times, as was customary in those days, and there I read the obituary notice of his death of a heart attack on November 3rd 1957. It was a brief and very formal notice. It was a paltry comment on an incredible life.

The following year (in June 1958) having planned a trip across Canada to Alaska, my friend Pat Findlay and I visited Orgonon, the site of Reich's institute. We saw his bust made by sculptress Jo Jenks and some faded flowers. Nearby were the scattered remains of Orgone Accumulators destroyed under the supervision of FDA inspectors. It was early morning and having only been there a few minutes, a vehicle came roaring down the track and we were chased away by his daughter Eva Reich, angrily accusing us of trespassing; it was not possible to talk to her. Our attempts to explain were cut short, and this only confirmed (if confirmation were necessary) the long-term tragedy and effects of a life and research career cut short by misguided bureaucracy.

How could people react like that?

But it was not only the trial itself, but also how people reacted subsequently after the trial that shocked me the most. Before the FDA case mounted against him, most people in those artistic and creative circles had been so positive and enthusiastic about Reich and had his books in their libraries. But after Reich's arrest most seemed to lose interest. The general opinion was that if the USA Federal Authorities condemned something, then they must be right.

I did not see it that way. To me Reich's work was a powerful consideration of an alternate energy. At the time of his death I had experimented to the point that I had no doubt of the validity of his research.

I have now been talking and writing about Wilhelm Reich for over fifty years. Clearly I am not the only one. People still periodically contact me especially about the published text I wrote in Big Sur, California in 1964. It is somewhat of a surprise to me because this was privately published. In those days of what now seem like technological history, I hand mimeographed a limited edition of 400 copies for circulation to interested associates who came to the lecture I gave at the Esalen Institute. Somehow even Dr. Simeon Tropp who was with Dr. Reich during the crucial Oranur and cloud buster experiments (discussed in more detail in Chapter 7), obtained a copy and when he came to London three years later, in 1967, he contacted me; this was just the year before he died. That was an important visit for me. I was worried about the reaction generally to what I had written and he gave me a piece of advice that often comes back to me. With a wry smile he said to me, "Get yourself in a little trouble." Well I did. And so I have written and spoken about my ideas since that time, even being mocked for so doing.

This year (2007) is an especially important time to stand up and be counted as regards Reich, marking the fiftieth anniversary since his death. The Wilhelm Reich Foundation emailed me to say they were organising a special event. It started me thinking. Times are changing. There is no longer the blind belief that a government can do no wrong. Since those times there has been the debacle of the Vietnam War and the pre-emptive strike in Iraq is now seen as illegal as well as being a disaster. A recent documentary on the Discovery channel to mark the anniversary of the murder of Martin Luther King discussed how he was killed. It was said, in this programme, that J. Edgar Hoover - the former head of the FBI whose puritanical purges destroyed the lives of many creative people, was himself being blackmailed by the Mafia because he was (allegedly) a closet homosexual. Fifteen, maybe even ten years ago, they could not have said that in a TV documentary. Eventually the underlying truth comes out and I believe it will be so with Reich. One day his work will be accepted.

Despite the dismissal of Reich's work generally, over the years I continued to write about what happened to Reich and his research, waiting for signs of a reappraisal. I think that time is approaching. I am writing another book about my search to understand cosmic energies but that is a particular book and will probably only interest a limited few. I decided to write something about his work during this anniversary year. I felt it was imperative to write something that would interest people who do not necessarily know about Reich to help them see beyond the oft quoted view that he was either a fraud or deluded and to put aside all the myths, the slurs, the accusations and the dismissals and spark a fresh interest to read his own words and judge for themselves. For that was how I became interested.

Several people suggested that I should reissue the 1964 text of 'Cosmic Metabolism and Vortical Accretion', but though still valid, it is a historical piece Also my own thinking and understanding has expanded since then, but always with great respect for the insight Reich had.

So this essay is my own tribute to Reich to show how his work influenced my thinking. I have compiled a selection of short pieces from what I had written in 1964, in 1979 and most recently, this year in 2007, It is a testament of what I have learned over the last fifty years that includes the truth, as I see it, of what Reich found, as a scientist, as a seeker after facts, no matter at what cost; a man with profound insight.

You too will need to keep an open mind about what happened to him if you are going to focus on what his writings have to offer.

Chapter 2. The Conclusions I came to about Reich's Findings on Energy:
The Cosmos is not 'out there', but linked to us

"We are all in the gutter but some of us are looking at the stars"
                                                                Oscar Wilde

Fascinated by the stars

Even as a child the stars fascinated me. In those days, the early nineteen thirties, street lighting was far less intense and in outer London suburbia, the stars were very visible in the dark night sky. Pollution was far less than today, and apart from certain industrial areas, was seldom a topic of concern. I read a number of books about astronomy and mused about this reality, seemingly forever out of reach. Books on astronomy, although lacking the colour illustrations and popularisation of current astronomical literature, provided a much more open debate of how the cosmos came to be. There was no impression that research was in its final state – as is so often implied in today's books. For example in those early books there was no concept of the so called 'big bang' - now presented as an inalienable and unchallengeable fact when, in fact, it is a very debatable and unproven opinion.

There was still debate in the nineteen forties and fifties and that was the foundation for my thinking on astronomy. As I later discovered, there has been a hardening of opinion by professional astronomers about present day cosmological conceptions. This has been rather like political opinion, taking sides; one side supports the 'big bang' concept and the other the so-called 'steady state' concept. I even need to explain now what a 'steady state' means, so much has the 'big bang' theory become popularised. In contrast the 'steady state' argument is that the cosmos has always existed and although there have been continuous changes the overall structure is steady; new stars form, old ones die but these do not affect the overall reality. The 'big bang'/ 'steady state' opining has hardly been scientific. Astronomers could and have argued endlessly – unable to prove the other wrong. Technology has meant visits to local space (not yet even to the outer reaches of the solar system), and space telescopy has given us far more detailed observations, but these have not provided basic insight that would settle this argument. Though seldom admitted, what has occurred is a consolidation of opinion in favour of the 'big bang' theory, effectively extinguishing debate. Consolidation of opinion is a political reality, not science. It is important not to be overawed by the certainty given to some opinions about science and astronomy. We need to be aware that for astronomy in particular a lot is not practically provable - nobody could actually visit deep space and find out!

None of this closing down of the debate was apparent to me when as a young man I went to live in New York. I was in my early twenties and still openly interested in astronomy and what was out there in the cosmos. Living in New York I built a large reflecting telescope, grinding and polishing the mirror for it. Jazz drummer Jeff Morton, who, as I said earlier, introduced me to Reich's writings, also helped me build the telescope. I kept abreast of current scientific research through the *Scientific American* monthly and also by another popular but serious publication *Sky and Telescope* to which I subscribed for many years. In my Riverside Drive apartment I had access to the roof. This gave a clear view of the heavens with little of the sky obscured by other buildings. However the city lights made deep sky viewing difficult, but we often used the scope to view the moon and planets such as Venus, Jupiter and Saturn.

Jazz vibraphonist Lennie Cuje, now living and playing in Washington D.C., recently reminded me of a time in the early nineteen fifties when a group of musician friends came over to play. Afterwards, I invited everyone up to the roof with this telescope to look at the moon[4]. In our excitement, we had forgotten to prop open the door to the roof and then discovered that we had imprisoned ourselves on the roof as the door had closed behind us. The only way down was via a rickety fire escape. I would not leave my telescope up there. It was very precious to me. It was also large – the tube was 8ft long. It took three of us to carry it down the fire escape. This excited attention in a neighbouring building and we were then greeted by the police who were convinced we were burglars!

The expansive culture of New York in the 50's

As you can see, during the nineteen fifties I was still very involved in astronomy, but those years in New York also brought an entirely new set of influences. It was a very expansive culture; there were new influences in painting, sculpture, and poetry and above all, for me, the influence of Wilhelm Reich. There were many contemporary writers that we were interested to read, such as D.H. Lawrence (whose book "Lady Chatterley's Lover" was banned in the UK) and Henry Miller (at that time most of his writings were forbidden in the USA) that were challenging the status quo. As for visual art, the Museum of Modern Art was a favourite visiting place, but what has become a lasting influence for me was an exhibition of Van Gogh's work. It was the largest exhibition ever held and visited various US cities - Chicago, St Louis, Los`Angeles and Philadelphia. It was in Philly in February 1953 that I went to see it. There had been a big snowstorm - leaving a foot of snow on the ground. Seeing the panorama of canvases, especially the vibrant work of his time in Arles In the Provence was enthralling - so much so that on leaving the Museum the site of the snow came as a shock despite the fact that I had walked through the snow to get to the exhibition.

Reich had pointed out that Van Gogh depicted the energy movement that he described as bio-energy and that was what Van Gogh painted. It is so

---

[4] As Sue reminded me while I was writing this, I still do try to get people to look at the sky. Recently we had people around for dinner in France and before dessert I took everyone out into the road to look at the moon while our neighbour who had prepared a beautiful tarte tatin waited patiently to serve it. This is in a way a belated apology!

clearly shown in his painting "Starry Night". That was what has always inspired me about Van Gogh's paintings - the way he conveyed the reality of energy.

It was a really exciting time of being open to new ideas. I had already started reading Freud's writings before I went to New York, while working on the Queen Mary making trips to New York. I followed that by studying Reich in New York. As I mentioned the first book I read was 'The Function of the Orgasm'. Jeff Morton lent it to me because I had been talking about Freud's work as revelatory. Initially I was hesitant to read someone that would not have the picture that Freud had. But as I read Reich it made me realise that this was a direct continuation of what Freud had realised about the libido. It is now a commonly used term but at that time this idea of libido as the sexual energy, which motivated people, was new. Originally in the late 19th century, the French psychologist Charcot knew that the problem with hysterical paralysis was caused by sexual repression. His remark while treating a woman with this kind of paralysis substantially influenced Freud's career. In an aside to other doctors including Freud, Charcot remarked, "We all know what cures this - penis normalis dosim repetur". At that time sexual desire and satisfaction was just not talked about openly.

This seemingly casual observation was what gave Freud the impetus to investigate neurosis as sexual repression. He developed the concept of the libido that eventually won recognition, by successfully treating hysterical paralysis, based on this understanding. In fact it was his ability to help a female member of the Austrian royal family that had brought Freud in from the cold with his theories. Until that time Freud had worked alone for ten years, virtually ostracised by his medical colleagues. Freud said that eventually someone would come along and be able to demonstrate the chemical basis for the libido. That was where Reich eventually succeeded. But it turned out that the libido did not have a chemical basis but it was a blockage of psycho/sexual energy that gave rise to neurosis.

The Influence of Reich

Reich explained in "The Function of the Orgasm" that freeing sexual energy through complete orgasm was the key to a genuine cure of neurosis. His book "The Sexual Revolution" described the results of this change of awareness. He was the pioneer of the sexual revolution although he is rarely - maybe apart from the film "W.R - Mysteries of the Orgasm", given due credit.

What Reich discovered is that neurosis is not only psychological but also physical; in fact the energy of the libido becomes locked into the musculature - the entire muscular system of the body. His book Character Analysis, which was the second book I read, describes neurosis in terms of resistance as a means of blocking unpleasant (even traumatic) experiences. Freud had originally introduced the term 'resistance' as a central concept of his approach to psychoanalysis. It is the conscious desire to be free of a neurosis countered by the unconscious fear of what would happen if that neurosis were dissolved. Freud tried to unlock this using the method of free association, whereby the patient was encouraged to say whatever came immediately into his or her mind when given a specific word. Reich was also concerned with a somatic approach to unlocking resistance.

His book "Character Analysis" mapped out the validity of using the method of character analysis for unravelling neurosis. The book describes Reich's success in treating this. He took a very different approach, working physically with the patient, which was contrary to the classic image of psychoanalysts passively listening while the patient on the couch talks.

My view of the world of humanity became identified with the work of these two men - Freud and Reich. However it was from reading Reich's books that convinced me to begin psychotherapy - believing I could greatly improve my life by doing so. It was not that I felt in desperate need of therapy. In those days many people in New York, who did not consider themselves particularly neurotic, believed that their perception of life could be improved by therapy. Today therapy is almost like an appendage or an attachment to a must-have life style, particularly in New York. It was not like that in the fifties - then it was more of a search for personal insight.

For a brief time I visited one of the twenty doctors trained by Reich - Dr. Handelman - but his treatment was expensive and on my budget I could only afford infrequent visits. By this time Lennie Tristano's brother, Michael - who was a trained psychologist, moved from Chicago to New York and his fees were more modest. So I began a treatment that lasted several years.

Reichian therapy entailed Freudian free association, but also included breathing combined with physical therapy to loosen what Reich termed 'muscular armouring'. That helped me to gain insight into the connection between thoughts and muscular tension and the connection of physical and mental aspects in terms of energy.

After reading "Character Analysis", I then read "The Cancer Biopathy". This book discusses how cancer results from the severe blocking of bio-energy. I will discuss in detail in Section 2 how Reich elaborated his discoveries, through experiments, of bions and atmospheric energy identical to the energy of life within us. But what was significant to me about this writing at the time was his conclusion about the movement of this energy as spiral. This spiral movement is so key in nature. Blood flows through the arteries in a spiral way. The movement of protoplasm, the living material that we are all made of and which is the structure of living organisms from the simplest to the most complex, even DNA, reflects the spiral nature of energy movement. This spiral nature is manifest in cloud formation and movement, in storms such as hurricanes and tornados. In fact a spiral movement is universal; it is the way in which our globe, the solar system and process of planets, stars and galaxies rotate around each other all manifesting spiral movement. Reich described this process as 'Orgonomic Functionalism' and discussed this in detail in his book "Cosmic Superimposition". For me that was the breakthrough of making the connection between life as we know it and the life energy that is all around us - the orgone energy as Reich described it. It also helped me to understand energy in a different way, as a spiral process.

Reich's concept of orgone energy

I will discuss orgone energy in more technical detail in Section 2 but I need at least to introduce Reich's concept of orgone energy here. The orgone energy concept has unfortunately led to much misunderstanding, not least the idea that orgone is some magical, previously unknown substance or energy. It is not that. It became clear to me that Reich used that term to describe phenomena from many diverse sources, phenomena that had been dismissed as only this or only that. The fundamental difference of classical science and Reich's work is that he was always searching for the common denominator that linked previously separate disciplines. He described this as 'the common functioning principle' in "Cosmic Superimposition". So much of scientific investigation looks at scientific evidence from within very particular boundaries of say chemistry or biology. These seem to become welded into demarcating positions, sometimes even denying other findings. As an illustration, since Pasteur, the concept of spontaneous generation has been dismissed as a delusion persisting from the middle ages. Though Pasteur succeeded in sealing foodstuff in sterile and airtight containers, and preserving food in this way, such preservation does not last forever. However, no matter how careful such preparations are made, bio-degeneration eventually sets in. Degeneration of foodstuff is classically attributed to "air germs". Clearly there are no air germs in hermetically sealed experiments. Such an explanation hides a plethora of phenomena and as Reich pointed out in "The Cancer Biopathy" no one has seen these 'air germs'. But this idea persists as though in viable.

Reich's research led to a clear scientific conclusion that everything has a unifying principle, in fact it has an energy field and this is not the expansive energy of fire. Our preoccupation with the energy that powers our machines has overlooked the energy of contraction or condensation. This is life-giving energy; it is what vitalises the living. This is what he describes as orgone energy. Similar conclusions have been reached in various cultures. For example, Chinese medicine is based on understanding the 'chi'- the life energy that flows through the body. The Indian conception is also of a life/cosmic force known as "prana". Western culture has tended to deride such concepts as though illusory. Only in recent years with the increasing popularity of "alternative" medicine, concepts of a fundamental life force are gaining credence. Reich conceptualised Orgone as the universal life energy throughout the cosmos.

Reich discovered how the energy potential of the atmosphere could be channelled and used to benefit health. Details of how Reich discovered that such an assemblage as an Orgone Accumulator increases the energy potential of the atmosphere and how living beings, animals and humans can benefit from this energy enhancement are described simply in his books, particularly in "The Cancer Biopathy". I built several of these accumulators, and became familiar with the effects of these and other orgone devices; I began to understand the unity of functioning that he had so graphically described. I will discuss the accumulator in more detail in Section 2 but it can be simply described as follows. The Orgone Accumulator is a box of alternate layers of metallic and non-metallic matter, with the outer layer of non-metallic material and the final inner layer of metallic matter. The principle of energy accumulation is that non-metallic matter absorbs the energy and metallic matter attracts it and then repels it again. The overall effect is that the metal draws the energy from the non-metallic matter, part of which it reflects back and part of which reflects through to the next layer. A box constructed in this way results in a higher energy level on the inside and can be beneficial to someone sat in the box. Such a device was also found to be beneficial to animals and plants.

The accumulator was not a new phenomenon. Indeed devices that act as accumulators are found in every home and workplace, such as refrigerators and most strikingly house insulation, particularly insulation made of mineral wool and backed with metal foil. What Reich realised was the fundamental significance of accumulating energy. I will discuss this in more detail in Chapter 4, concerning the Oranur experiments that Reich undertook.

Here I want to emphasise that Orgone then is not some previously unknown substance but ever present energy that humanity has ignored or explained as isolated phenomena. The significance of this process of accumulation of energy is that it goes against a generally accepted law of science. This is discussed in detail in Section 2 but I need to introduce it here as an important aspect of Reich's findings on energy. In science, the second law of thermodynamics states that all energy proceeds from the higher level to the lower. Just think about it. When the petrol in the engine of our cars is fired it provides a continuous series of mini-explosions; this is what I mean by expansive energy. It is the same in rockets and in jet turbines and if we look at the steam turbine it is the same process. It is expansive. From that process of expansion was derived the concept of the second law of thermodynamics. All the energies of fire, upon which our culture depends, use the energy within matter and in a burning process, which is expansive. The burning process goes from burning at an intense level to a low level. This second law of thermodynamics, known also as the law of entropy, states that energy can only proceed in this way, from a high level of intensity to a low level of intensity. What Reich's Orgone Accumulator, discussed in "The Cancer Biopathy" showed, is that the reverse of this also takes place. Energy can be accumulated and can increase in intensity.

I began experimenting

Having built some accumulators I then built what Reich described in "The Oranur Experiment" as a DOR (Deadly Orgone energy) buster. The life energy can become stale and this is the root of the disease process - hence the term Deadly Orgone or DOR energy. This came out of his realisation that you can ground the energy, somewhat similar to a lightning rod. The lightning rod is passive but should a charge of lightning strike a building it runs harmlessly through the rod and does not inflict damage on the building or people around. In contrast to the rod the DOR buster is a series of metal tubes placed in a container of water. Reich discovered that as metal attracts and draws the energy then water absorbs it. Such a device placed in a room helps to clear it of stale energy. We are already familiar with such a process. We accept that the burning of incense has a purification effect, although this works from a different standpoint.

For a long time I hesitated to go further. I knew, from Reich's writing, that a larger version of the DOR Buster could have an effect in terms of helping to clean the weather. But to go outside with a huge array of copper pipes pointing at the sky was another matter. Imagine doing that in downtown Manhattan in 1961. Imagine what J Edgar Hoover would have made of something like that.

I regularly held jam sessions in my downtown loft. One night, in 1960, everyone had left except one saxophonist – Vince Bottari and we were talking about the DOR Buster. I had purchased a number of copper pipes at that stage. He said to me, "Do you want to try and see if the pipes can affect the weather?" So we assembled a rather crude version of a cloudbuster and pointed it out of this seventh storey window. After a few minutes we saw a brownish aura forming around the end of the tubes, clearly visible against an early dawn sky. And we were not on drugs or alcohol or anything else!

Suddenly there was a little breeze and this was in a hot oppressive summer time night. We both said, "Did you feel that? Then the breeze died down and nothing seemed to happen. It is not surprising that doubts set in. We were not convinced. Having decided to go to the beach we left. Taking the subway to Brighton beach. On arriving I had not noticed that the sky was beginning to clear. Later when we went to take the elevated subway back we saw huge thunderhead clouds over Manhattan, while Brighton beach was clear. By the time we got out of the train at Houston Street, in Lower Manhattan, it was raining like a cloudburst. I left Vince and went back to the apartment. It had occurred to me by then that our seemingly innocuous experiment might have had an effect. We had not dismantled the pipes before we left. When I got to the loft studio I could see heat waves within the room. The room was 60 feet long and there were these heat waves like you see in the desert. I really started to feel scared. I had never experienced anything like this. I rushed across the room. I remember being fearful that I might have a heart attack. It was that frightening. I pulled the pipes in and quickly closed the window. I went up to the roof. Above and to the south the sky was clear but immediately above me and to the north a pile of huge thunderhead clouds were gathered, as though I was standing on the very spot of the demarcation of a storm and clear sky. I phoned the Weather Bureau and there was no mention of a storm – only a forecast of high humidity and heat.

People might say - so what, just a storm over Manhattan!

It was much later after further experimentation that I realised this had not been an accident. But if I had not had that initial experience I probably would not have gone any further, maybe I would not have become so convinced of what I now know to be true.

I kept experimenting and reading. I was trying to figure out the relationship of nuclear energy and orgone energy. For me it was a consideration of seeing how these separate aspects of reality were interlinked. Reich had shown that orgone energy was condensative in principle – in other words it was formative energy, drawn down from the atmosphere, from space. That is how, for example, seeds start to grow. This energy forms into living matter while, in contrast, nuclear energy is the ultimate in expansive energy. Consider how the mushroom cloud from a nuclear explosion expands and expands out, breaking down all life in its path. The entire city of Hiroshima was virtually dust after the atom bomb, as shown in the pictures.

One day I was in my loft, studying and trying to figure out this dilemma of DOR energy, nuclear energy and the life energy – orgone energy as Reich described it. How did they relate to each other? And suddenly I realised how they linked together – how we on Earth and the cosmos are interconnected. I was thinking about DOR deadly radiation energy and the radiation from the Sun. We used to see the Sun as a burning chemical furnace. With the development of nuclear energy, the conception of solar radiation changed and the astronomical theory then viewed the Sun as a nuclear furnace. What struck me is that when the energy coming from the sun has travelled 93 million miles it becomes relatively benign and plays a vital role in our own and the Earth's health. The deadly radiation from the surface of the Sun expands into Space and in so doing it is transformed and becomes benign.

This fact, though unquestioned has great significance. I realised that Space is the modulator transforming the expansive solar radiation into the benign energy that reaches us. It has a function of allowing dead/waste energy to reach a maximum point of dispersion and as it does so the energy becomes condensative becoming life giving energy again.

It was the most incredible moment of my life when I realised that connection. I was so excited I got up and danced round the room!

Chapter 3. Developing ideas and building understanding – a difficult path

The difficulties of explaining new concepts

"The globe is the centre of a huge spiral of energy; it doesn't turn from explosive energy but from spiral energy. Space becomes seen not as a void but as a function and energy has to travel through deep space to regenerate"
(Peter Ind, Interview with Ena Kendall for Observer Magazine, 16th August 1992)

Understanding how the earth and the cosmos interlink was one thing, trying to explain that or have it accepted has been quite another.

I have indicated how Reich had a profound influence on my life as a young man but for me it did not stop there. I continued to read what he said, undertake some of his simpler experiments and read very widely about the cosmos, scientific thinking and debates about energy. I also continued to write about this and have included in this essay some excerpts of my earlier writing that not only discussed Reich's work but also my own thinking about cosmology. It has been a lifetime of study. One of the themes that struck me the more I read about orthodox astronomy was this perspective that the cosmos is out there, we are here and there is seemingly no link. My search was to understand the cosmos – it could not just be empty space "out there".

The more I read and thought, the more it became clear to me that we are bogged down by the idea of the cosmos as something separate from us. But the common theme to the excerpts that are included here is showing how we here on earth, and the cosmos are interconnected. In a way this selection of writings shows the search that led to an understanding.

Developing that understanding required keeping an open mind, even when others were dismissive, critical, derogatory, (or all three!), about what I saw as some simple facts. Peoples' reactions have been interesting. The more I learned the more it seemed to contradict what I was led to believe and the more dismissive people would be. Why?

I have come to the conclusion that what I learnt goes against the grain of what is commonly taught about science and the cosmos. It is not that the concepts I put forward are <u>that</u> complex. It is merely that they are different. Are we still going to stick to the stubborn belief about the sun rising and setting rather than recognising that the earth rotates continually?

What I have realised in the reactions to these writings is that if people begin to question their own accepted perspective it often gives rise to anxiety; even severe anxiety. To look at so many things in a different way is very difficult. So before looking at these excerpts (in Sections 2 and 3) that focus on a discussion of the energy potential that we ignore, it is important to explain what a difficult path it can be to develop a different understanding.

Writing in 1964 - Open and hopeful

Section 2 of this essay is an excerpt from the original 1964 publication of Cosmic Metabolism and Vortical Accretion, *written in Big Sur, California when I lived there in the 1960's. But the ideas for that book started while I was still living in New York. They began with the reflection of the conflict I had felt about what had happened to Reich. Everything that Reich had learnt and described in his work was clearly apparent to me. Here was a great internationally acclaimed scientist accused of alleged fraud and then jailed for contempt of court. It did not make sense.*

After I read Wilhelm Reich's book "Cosmic Superimposition" in 1954 I started to write about what I had learned but my early writing was somewhat fragmentary. I was struggling with the concepts of universal functioning presented in that book. Even though the editors of his "Selected Writings" described them as hypothetical, they could be nothing but the truth if his discoveries in Orgone physics were indeed factual.

Having moved to California in 1963 and no longer just involved in the jazz scene, I started a new life. This was the time to write about what I had learned. We were living in a small wooden house – the Goat House – that I made habitable, one thousand feet above the Pacific with a view across the ocean; having that vast background of mountains behind; the ocean in front of me and the vast panorama of unpolluted sky above.

A particular issue of the Scientific American journal at that time dealt exclusively with cosmological concepts and many fine astronomical photos were reproduced in it. Pondering over a photo of a barred spiral galaxy - one of the enigmas of astronomy - I suddenly understood how the barred spiral had evolved. This flash of insight, accompanied by much strong emotion, convinced me that I had to continue.

By this stage it was more than simply reiterating what Reich had achieved and musing on the tragic end to his life. I wrote Cosmic Metabolism as a combination of what Reich had discovered, confirming its reality and adding what I had learned. I called the understanding that I had come to 'Cosmic Metabolism', which I initially discussed in the frontispiece. Reich never used that concept but it was his work that led me to these further conclusions about energy.

In 1964 I felt that I had the world in front of me. I was married and we had a new young family, we had moved out to the sunshine and clean air of Big Sur, I was seeing myself, especially after my New York life, as part of an expanding world, but at the same time I could not get anywhere with what I had learned so it was doubly frustrating. It was so difficult to accept what had happened to Reich, especially when I had such respect for his work. The terrible shock of the treatment meted out to him as though he was some back street medical con man rather than an internationally recognised doctor and psychiatrist was still with me even seven years later. Personally I was also struggling with trying to gain some recognition. Although I was in my thirties how was I going to get some kind of means of surviving in a culture that seemed to be a total rejection of what I had learnt as a jazz musician, to say nothing about what I had learned about the cosmos? To develop as a jazz musician requires considerable skill, knowledge as well as talent. As many musicians have stated, the time and study they put in is at least equivalent to that of a medical doctor and at the end there is likely to be a minimum of recognition and little employment. I had learnt so much about the energy that is around us and used that insight creatively not only in my playing but also in my painting. So writing in 1964, I felt the need to set it down; somehow to put some very different thoughts 'out there'.

But it was not easy. Those days were long before the Internet was even conceived and unless one was a recognised academic, it was not always possible to access specialised information or be seen to have knowledge outside the academic arena. I believed then that by comparing Reich's work with orthodox astronomical concepts, my re-evaluation would have some positive impact upon academic thought. I began to understand how the revolution in thinking brought about by Reich was too challenging to the limitations of academic thought as it was in those times. I learned the hard way. I will discuss this in more detail in Chapter 6.

My naiveté, in 1964, was simply the expectation that those concepts would make some kind of an impact at that time. I know that eventually Reich's work will have impact, either because people become aware of the significance of his findings or future generations will independently come to a similar understanding.

And I was naïve. Following the publication of my book "Cosmic Metabolism and Vortical Accretion" an employee of the Rand Corporation visited me in Big Sur[5]. It was seven years after Reich's death. This man, Dr. Charles Kelley, had been at one time an associate of Reich's. Eight years after the trial that led to his jailing and death in jail, the US government were nevertheless still extremely interested in his discoveries. Kelley quizzed me about what I might know regarding gravity. Sensing danger I played dumb – and eventually he left.

n 1966 I left California and returned to the UK. I felt disillusioned about the lack of genuine scientific interest in Reich's concepts and cosmic energy. Then in 1967, Doctor Simeon Tropp (as I have already mentioned, one of Reich's close colleagues) coming to see me gave me a boost in the conviction that I was not wrong in what I had concluded. But I needed to earn a living. I tried to find a way through by teaching, by releasing the

---

[5] I was interested to see Jane Fonda's recent description about the Rand Corporation in her book "Jane Fonda: My Life So Far" (2005)

1979 – In a cosmically blind world: a bleak time

recordings I had made in New York and eventually doing the odd tour. The tours were also frustrating, even though they were with the musicians that I had previously had a rapport with. Jazz had become commercial and competitive. The camaraderie of those early days of jazz in New York had gone.

The music tours I did, mainly around Europe, had been somewhat disappointing but I had managed to save some money and I bought a very run down house in a London suburb in 1976. I had to rent out every space I could just to meet bank payments, working all hours to improve it but at least I had a place of my own. My marriage was over, my wife had the house in Wales and I had to start afresh. I was not with my children, which was very hard. I was trying to write in between trying to earn a living. It was a very testing time.

By 1979 I had gone through all the hard work of trying to find a way forward. I had re-established my recording studio (this time in London). However 1979 was also the year when I realised that my hopes of getting ideas about energy across were not going to be realised soon. It was frustrating. Leaving California and returning to England, was effectively returning to the place I had escaped from in the early 50's. And nothing seemed to have changed. There was no expansion, nothing, in the thinking. There was this idea of swinging London, but there was nothing swinging about it as far as I was concerned - it was hype. It all felt shallow, shabby and false.

But I knew that whatever was happening in my life I had realised something significant. It was a very difficult time to get really different concepts across. The whole idea of alternative thinking and opening up with a new era – the concept of the Age of Aquarius, which had surfaced in the 50's and by the 60's had become fashionable, had gone by the 1970's. The terrible Vietnam War had been very disillusioning. There had been bad economic times. The chances of getting any really new ideas moving seemed remote. Whether I was able to do anything with it or not, I wanted these ideas down in print. So, amidst all the playing, building works and creating a recording studio, I wrote a synopsis of what I had learned.

This 1979 essay (Section 3 is an extract of this) was a statement that this was my contribution from what I had learned. It was not denying Reich's work but when I sent a copy to the Reich Institute, as it was then, I was rebuffed, claiming that I had just appropriated his work. This was untrue. When that happened it only reaffirmed that there seemed no way in – no way for this to be accepted – except for me to say that I had written it and it was true. I had it printed and put some copies out. It was not like the time in Big Sur, where I had given a lecture at Esalen and raised money for the publication. In 1979 I just gave copies to friends and musicians who were interested. People like musician Bernie Cash; he was supportive but he was struggling too. He had finally got his PhD on the jazz saxophonist, Lester Young, but that combined with continually trying to earn a living in jazz, had obviously taken a toll on his health.

I tried to get this synopsis published but no one at that time was interested in Reich or when there was some interest the potential publisher wanted me to write it in a commercial way. (Even in the late 90's when I sent a summary to the Bloomsbury Press and they took me to lunch and commended the writing, they said there was no chance for a publication on Reich). But at least in 1979 I published it.

It seemed a very bleak period to me and society seemed closed down even more on anything that was not about economic growth. I made contact with people involved in alternative groups or discussions but they appeared to be concerned only with their own contributions to thought. There was not the excitement and the sharing of ideas as I had found in New York in the 50's and 60's. Nor was it like the meeting with Simeon Tropp in '67. That was exciting because he had been there working with Reich. When he came he saw me as someone somehow carrying the flag and that was so supportive. Often people discussing any alternatives would sort of pat me on the head and say yes that's interesting but have you seen what so and so is doing; they seemed to be focused on the next thing. Like Swinging London, they were on to the new vogue, "something that counts". But I knew my writing was valid- for some time in the future.

It is ironic. It had been unfashionable to talk about Reich and his ideas in America in the 1960s for one set of reasons - he was seemingly discredited. But in the UK by the late seventies it had become unfashionable for another set of reasons - Reich was then considered old hat and people were only interested in the 'latest thing'.

What could I do? What I did was to talk about the ideas contained in the 1979 essay in a whole series of interviews. If I look back at some of those interviews, it was always so hard to get my cosmological writing taken seriously as part of my life, rather than an addition:

> "..when time permits he is also working on a third book called *Cosmic Metabolism.*" (Peter Ind: An interview with Gordon Jack, Jazz Journal June 1996)

But sometimes writers would cover these ideas in more detail; I hoped even their interest in Reich I hoped could be raised by my mentioning them:

> "Peter Ind is often regarded as a 'maverick' as though that prevented the creation of a mass of solid achievement. Currently he is writing on cosmology and 'aspects of science that have been sidelined', with a determination to get his writings in order, with the aim of publication. It is without a sense of self-pity that he says he sees a parallel between his own career and scientists

> like Tesla and Reich who achieved much without recognition. Conversation with Peter Ind sent Jazz Rag staff scurrying to encyclopaedias …..As to Wilhelm Reich, a disciple of Freud and innovator of rather eccentric theories of energy, he was indeed put in prison (where he died) and his books burned in 1950's America. Peter Ind's sense of solidarity with such characters is very much a piece of his uncompromising approach to music"
> Interview The Jazz Rag Jan/Feb 1999.

If I could not get these ideas published, at least it meant that more people had heard of Reich. Sometimes they did see the interconnection of my music and my understanding of life and even understood some of Reich's work:

> "Ind's metaphysical studies and writings have influenced his bass playing. 'In New York in the 50's there was a lot of interest in psychology among musicians and artists. Many went to Freudian shrinks, but many studied Wilhelm Reich', Ind says of the controversial researcher who proclaimed the existence of orgone energy, developed orgonomy to study the mysterious force, and invented the Orgone Accumulator to capture it. 'Reich's work led him far beyond psychiatry and into human experimentation, and I decided to experiment myself'. Ind gathered his findings in the 64 book 'Cosmic Metabolism and Vortical Accretion' and he plans to publish a revised version."
> (Peter Ind: Bass Metaphysics Interview with John Goldsby *Bass Player* Oct 2000)

Time and again I said that you cannot talk about my music without asking me about my philosophy of life. Rarely did someone get it right but the article in the Observer magazine is the one I still appreciate.

> "His philosophical musings led him to propose his own theory of cosmic function, which he develops in a long paper (which she had read) Cosmic Metabolism and Vortical Accretion (1979) 'We have built a picture of a cosmos that somehow was swept into motion by a huge explosion and that will run down,' he explains. 'It is to do with the explosive side of reality and we have not yet taken on board that there are other aspects of energy that could be tapped. I am not the only person to see an alternative understanding but the snag is it leaves one outside the culture. The globe is the centre of a huge spiral of energy; it doesn't turn from explosive energy but from spiral energy….' Acceptance of his concepts, he argues, would help us to come to grips with the problems of pollution, applying 'cosmic engineering principles' to tackle it and drawing fresh cosmic energy from space. Methods of doing this have already been explained but have been overlooked by orthodox science…..
> For those of us who are not just agnostic but downright baffled

by black holes and white holes, big bangs and neutron stars, and above all by Dr Stephen Hawking, the idea that a man playing the bass two nights a week at an East End jazz club might have worked out the secret of the universe is just what we need."

A room of my own: Peter Ind Interview by Ena Kendall Observer Magazine 16th August 1992

To see some comment in print was at least gratifying and I continued writing about and promoting Reich. At least by 2005 I had a chapter in the Jazz Visions book where I could talk about Reich's influence on the jazz and art scene in New York in the 1950's and 60's. I had been able to show the link. But there was still the frustration of knowing that Reich's work was not given due recognition.

2007 - Still living in hope but older, wiser and not deluded by 'green' behaviour

Since the late 70's it has been apparent that Reich has been seen as old fashioned or he has been dismissed or ignored. In that respect very little appears to have changed in the fifty years since his death. The vast majority of young people appear not to know that he even existed.

By the Millennium I was writing about Reich and his continuing (although unrecognised) contribution, discussed in Section 4, but also how his thinking provides a different reflection on issues of global warming, environmental pollution and sources of renewable energy. Natural disasters like the Tsunami and manmade disasters such as the Iraq conflict and the need for easily obtainable oil have added fresh reflections on environmental pollution.

There is a larger story to tell about cosmic energy generally and Reich's influence but for this publication I have pulled out some excerpts about Cosmic Metabolism, fire energy and the search for renewable energy sources (in Sections 2 and 3). This needs to be a key element of our discussions about the environment and global warming and it is not!

Here, considering how to present ideas, I want to highlight some key concerns for me in my 2007 writing. Firstly, in late 2006 there seemed to be a seed change in outlook regarding climate change. This has been spearheaded by the film and the book produced by former US presidential candidate Al Gore. (As an interesting aside, I was part of the jazz group playing in London at the launch of Gore's book about climate change, where free copies were being given to those who attended the launch. I asked if I could have one but as a lowly jazz musician I was not seen as worthy enough to receive a freebie!)

The endeavours leading toward a change in reducing the amount of pollution are certainly laudable. However, as I see the situation, while we continue to rely for most of our energy needs upon fossil fuels there will be little impact upon climate change. Even if we succeed in reducing the carbon imprint by 30% - a very optimistic target – we will have modified the environmental impact hardly at all. I have no wish to decry such efforts, but my pessimism in this regard is twofold. Firstly no matter how diligently the world tries to tackle global warming from this standpoint alone it will not lead to a solution. World population continues to grow, and as affluence increases globally, the increase in demand for products, for travel and for personal comforts and the burden upon industry to supply increasing demand will nullify the current attempts to reduce pollution. Though I wish it were otherwise I can only foresee an exponential increase in pollution and the ensuing negative effect upon climate change unless we tackle it from a different perspective.

Secondly, the accepted outlook regarding energy is basically faulty. Implicit in our concept of energy is that it is mainly an aspect of combustion. Though wind power, tidal power, solar power and other hydroelectric sources do supply some of our energy needs there are also those who feel the answer lays in nuclear energy. This is a very hazardous form of combustion – even though it may not be so obvious. But by exploiting nuclear reactions we are only storing trouble in the form of nuclear pollution for eons to come. The error lies in the belief that (apart from harnessing wind, water or solar power) energy as we produce it is of necessity a by-product of combustion.

Similarly with gravitation – we may not yet understand what such energies are, and we may not as yet know how to harness them but they are natural forces. Only a tiny amount would supply us with all the energy needs for the entire human population. Take travel for example – the energy needs for travel are considerable – but huge amounts of fossil fuels are used just to overcome inertia and gravity. Gravity is something that we should be learning to understand, not expending fossil fuels to overcome. However before we can even take an unbiased look at energies that do not involve fire energy, we need to change our conception that energy of necessity involves combustion. To launch a new conception of energy means firstly overcoming the prejudice surrounding the belief that only fossil fuels can produce energy in the quantity we need. We need to think totally "out of the box" otherwise this different conception will only bounce from an iron wall of preconception. That is the first and possibly the greatest task – to instil a different concept of energy – energy that is limitless and does not depend upon finite sources of so-called fossil fuels.

General concern regarding climate change has only seriously manifested in the last few years, though many have for a long time been concerned but have not had the political clout or influence to command the serious attention now prevalent. Paradoxically my reaction to the current concern is little different than it has been for many years. Having realised the ultimate dangers of our present course for almost fifty years, I believe that the real danger is somewhat different than the fears that low lying areas of the globe will be overtaken by rises in sea levels. The melting of the arctic ice can have little effect upon sea levels as the majority of it floats on the Arctic Ocean. What we do not know is how the isostatic balance will be affected if and when the ice cover of Greenland and the Antarctic continent melts. Remarkably it is found that there is frozen vegetation at the bottom of many ice cores, so at some time in the past there must have been very different climatic conditions where today there is seemingly permanent and eternal ice cover.

Having studied the problem from a somewhat different viewpoint I believe that the increasing weather disturbances are caused mainly by atmospheric attempts to metabolise pollution. Hence more storms, hurricanes, tornadoes, and other freak weather conditions are caused by a natural process of metabolism - the weather being the means of purification. It is no accident that beautiful weather often follows the most disastrous of storms. There is much fearful talk of a tipping point, a point of no return, when the disturbances become so great that total planetary chaos reins. But the careful student of past history realises that incredible catastrophic activity has occurred during mankind's earthly existence yet the planet has each time recovered, though man's memory of such events has been virtually extinguished through fear. Those students of history who have written about such occurrences have not yet influenced the majority of humanity. Even the disastrous tsunami that caused such chaos in southern Asian shores just over two years ago is beginning to lose its psychic impact amongst those who lived in unaffected areas. Whether or not our present pollutive activity will trigger sudden and massive climate change - I cannot predict. My view is that life in this civilisation will become progressively harder as pollution increases, and the resulting climatic disruption will eventually (coupled with the increasingly difficult to access fossil fuels) force us to find another way. Though present efforts such as harnessing wind and waterpower are laudable - these won't provide the much sought after solution.

This is where the work of Wilhelm Reich needs re-examining. Puritanical America was so busy castigating his work - as though investigating the reality of sexuality was the work of the devil - that this destroyed an insight that ironically is the direction we need to take after we have learned the hard way that fossil fuel energy is a fool's paradise. Today, fifty years after Reich's death, his work seems all but forgotten. But in his writings lay the clues to this entirely different conception of energy. The cosmic energy - amazingly this is identical with the energy of life, and Reich dedicated the latter part of his life to elucidating the nature of life energy - only to realise that it is in fact the prime cosmic energy. Before he was so tragically and wrongfully imprisoned, he began to show the directions needed to harness this cosmic energy.

So it is time for you to reconsider and read what he wrote and what I have written about him and cosmic energy, rather than relying on the opinions of those who have for the past fifty years effectively destroyed his reputation! It is not the vilification of his discoveries alone that have given rise to this, but it is also the vision that came from his work that for many has been too frightening to contemplate. But as Reich predicted, eventually his work will be recognised. The crisis today of global pollution and climate change plus the coming crisis of scarcity of fossil fuel supplies will force us to make a major re-evaluation of the way we organise our lives. This is where the work of Reich and of Tesla will come into their own.

So far I have explained in summary what Cosmic Metabolism is. I have talked about Reich and how he influenced my life. I have chronicled how I read his works and began to experiment and what that led me to conclude. And I have explained how, since then, I have tried to find ways of explaining what to me seems simple but what to many others seems to be so challenging, even frightening and so often dismissed. All of this has led me at different times to write about Cosmic Metabolism.

And it is this writing I want to introduce now. In Section 2 I have included some excerpts from the original 1964 publication *"Cosmic Metabolism and Vortical Accretion"*. This extract in particular will help you to see what cosmic energy is and Reich's understanding of this Orgone energy.

Then in Section 3 I have included some of the essay I wrote in 1979. I have particularly tried to pick out a section that focuses on a detailed discussion about dissipative as well as expansive properties of energy.

Once you have read the original ideas, then is the time to discuss in Section 4 why there is a cultural blind spot about one aspect of energy and why I now think that the scientific community finds it so hard to be open to new ideas. And why Reich was beyond his time and I am still, at 79, writing about the significance of his research and how it needs to be acknowledged!

Section 2

Cosmic Metabolism and Vortical Accretion

Extract – From 1964 writing: Open and Enthusiastic

Chapter 4 – Extract from Cosmic Metabolism and Vortical Accretion (CMVA)[6]

Understanding cosmic energy

"Scientific theory is a contrived foothold in the chaos of living phenomena"
Wilhelm Reich

1. Reconsidering entropy: much of what we observe in the cosmos evidences growth and not dissipation

The importance of Reich's discoveries and experimentation

It was Reich's investigations into sexuality and in particular the orgastic function that led him to discover the energetic laws underlying the living, eventually to comprehend the reality of the cosmic life energy. It is the energy that functions within us and manifests as life and manifests beyond us as cosmic formative energy.

As he pointed out, the magnitude of such a concept is not merely a projection of an ego, but of the very nature of coming to grips with the fundamental cosmic reality.

Was Reich with his extraordinary awareness and vision – right? Is orthodox science then widely off base and lacking understanding into fundamental aspects of reality? Or is it the other way around?

Although orthodox science has revolutionised our understanding of materialism and incredibly transformed our world, it is still light years away from grasping the deeper cosmic realities. The fact that there is an underlying reality - manifested on the one hand as the living and on the other hand as cosmic function – and that this became part of a deeper understanding thanks to Reich's perseverance in elucidating life functions, especially the function of the orgasm – will eventually become generalised knowledge, though this might not even happen for generations or even centuries hence.

Looking back at past scientific achievements we can see that, from the viewpoint of Einstein – Newton's laws are correct but incomplete; so from the standpoint of Orgonomy, the relativistic theories of Einstein are also incomplete.

Reich's viewpoint was a unitary one. His discoveries led him to comprehend the prime creative force or energy from which all evolves - life and non-life. His discoveries point to no other interpretation than of a

---

[6] This extract is the first chapters of the book I wrote in 1964 in Big Sur, California - 'Cosmic Metabolism and Vortical Accretion'. Those who have read the original will notice that the only change is the loss of some introductory writing and the extensive use of headings to introduce the different sections, rather than the original chapter headings.

new scientific awareness of creation! This realisation; that all true artists and sages have intuitively divined throughout the ages, is no longer a deeply held conviction through feeling or instinct alone, but is now reinforced by a scientific evaluation of previously unrecognised factual evidence.

The majority of today's scientific inventions stem from the application of what can be termed the mechanistic branch of natural law. As Reich so clearly demonstrated, mechanistic reality is merely a branch of nature, it is not the prime but a secondary function of nature.

The need to reconsider the concepts of ultimate cosmic law

There are certain conceptions that when originally formulated so revolutionised thinking that they have been considered as ultimate cosmic law. Viewing them as absolute law has hindered research and contributed to the present day scientific confusion - many findings remain seemingly isolated, apparently random facts. The underlying reality of the cosmic energy once accepted will bring the isolated picture of the universe into focus.

Three key examples of hindering concepts are:

1/ The absolute belief in the Second Law of Thermodynamics - which states that energy (as in heat) cannot increase in potential and eventually reaches the point of ultimate dissipation, whereby it can no longer be useful to us. But such a description is merely a value judgement and consequently unscientific. It overlooks the cosmic function of dissipation and what place such dissipation has in the overall cosmic picture.

2/ The absolute speed of light. Postulating that this is a fixed limit beyond which we cannot know. The simplest and most obvious refutation of such a pronouncement is that the largest aggregations of stars – known as galaxies are so large that the speed at which light travels though fast (some 300,000 kilometres per second) could not be responsible for maintaining galactic form. Many galaxies, being in excess of 100,000 light years in diameter – light or other electromagnetic energies could not be the prime cohesive force, as is obvious. For the 100,000 years it takes light to "travel" by the time it reaches the outer galactic edges it could not possibly "know" whether the galactic edge from which it commenced its journey actually still existed. Thus the concept of an absolute velocity is relative and clearly it does not explain the power, force or energy that holds galaxies together. The organisation such as a galaxy can only be understood by the realisation that there are fields of energy that are vaster than that of light propagation. That doesn't mean that we know what such energy fields are – but it would be irrational to deny their existence.

3/ The Lorentz transformation is a theoretical concept derived from the first two. It is largely if not entirely hypothetical. The concept is that as the velocity of light is reached a material body shrinks in proportion to its speed (relative to another body). However there is little indication of scientific verification of this concept.

The second law of thermo-dynamics/ entropy as a relative rather than a universal truth

Returning to the first concept that of the absolute validity of the second law of thermo dynamics - this is clearly invalidated by osmosis. Osmosis is the ability of biological material to pass through a semi-permeable membrane. This is evident in digestive processes and is clear evidence of reverse entropy. Cosmologists ignore osmosis as unimportant and by continuing to maintain the second law of thermodynamics as though absolute, they imply that the cosmos is running down and eventually will result in an even energy potential everywhere, what has been termed the cosmic "heat death"[7]. Truly a universal stagnation. Whereas the entropy law may be universally valid in the mechanical realm, it should be obvious to everyone that it is not valid in the realm of living functioning. This fact and the phenomena of growth, both contradict the absolute validity of the law of entropy!

In attempts to bypass and avoid the obvious fact that entropy is only a relative and not universal truth the common explanation is that although locally (that is on planet earth) life seems to contradict the concept of absolute entropy, viewed say from the point of view of the solar system as a whole, the planet earth can only sustain life due to the fact of solar radiation. Of course solar radiation is itself dissipative and planet earth could not support life without the dissipative entropic solar radiation. This kind of argument bypasses the fact of the reverse entropy in living systems by subsuming it under the overall concept of entropy. This fallacious reasoning is merely a form of begging the question.

It will appear that many of the interpretations of dying stars or planets may not be correct after all - for much of what we observe in the cosmos evidences growth and not dissipation. I am not trying to claim that there is no dissipation in the cosmos - but merely to point out that although dissipation is a natural function it does not simply mean that the universe was created at some finite point in the past and ever since has been running down.

Growth as part of the life cycle

Many phenomena - not only in life but in the non-living also manifests growth as part of a cycle of birth, growth and subsequent decline. Sunspots; hurricanes; auroras; storms in general; clouds; even civilisations all manifest such cycles. In wave phenomena, individual waves may be followed through their birth, growth and death cycles, a number of them merge together forming "group waves" that persist even while individual

---

[7] The concept of 'heat death' is that, as the cosmos burns out from the supposed and mythical 'big bang' there will eventually occur an even temperature throughout the cosmos

members decline. Much can be learned about wave phenomena while flying over a lake or the sea. Water mirrors the cosmic influence by wave manifestation. This is not to confuse life with non-life but to recognise that the phenomena of birth, growth and final cessation is not restricted to life processes alone.

We should open our minds to the fact that the cosmos is not a one-way system that was once created in some kind of nuclear explosion following which all is in decline. I am cynically reminded of a sketch by a New York comic - called "A funny thing happened to me on the way to the grave"! To reiterate - to claim that individual "life cycles" (of whatever nature) are merely the exception that proves the rule; the rule being that everything is subject to the absolute law of entropy is nonsense. Entropy must be viewed not as an absolute but as one cosmic function amongst others.

The mechanistic thinking of cause and effect

The ideas and the investigational approach that we describe as 'science' originated with a mechanistic interpretation of 'cause' and 'effect', postulating that all cause stems from the physically greater, the effect consequently being manifested in the physically lesser. This is the essence of mechanistic thinking and such views do not admit that 'cause' can manifest from within! Thus the realm of the living remains essentially incomprehensible to the mechanistic thinker. Superficially the motorised devices that we have come to accept and have become totally reliant upon - might be conceived as 'working from within' but of course though clever and complex in design are no more than applications of mechanistic law. Even today there are those who believe that eventually computers will be able to predict everything! It is so easy to confuse mechanistic reality as though it embraces even that which is still unformed. Life however is fundamentally different - the most elementary amoeba has volition and thus choice - even though limited.

Before the cosmic energy becomes transformed into matter, volition is still present. Such realities as the absolute unpredictability of weather patterns are a manifestation of the volition underlying cosmic energy processes. It is no accident that the reality of the life energy was discovered by a psychiatrist and not by an atomic physicist - the latter being involved in unravelling the secrets of dead matter.

Reich's discovery of the prime formative life energy

The paradox between the religious man's concept of an all powerful God being the ultimate cause and the scientist's concept of an all powerful cosmos that functions through mechanistic principles is resolved with Reich's discovery of the prime formative life energy (that which he termed Orgone). Whether or not we ultimately decide to use the term Orgone or some other appellation is not of importance. What is of importance is that we learn to understand the reality of Reich's discoveries

To return to the stubborn scientific belief - that of the absolute validity of the second law of thermodynamics - consider for a moment the largest material condensation of which we have clear evidence - that of a stellar galaxy. These are believed to be stars radiating away their energies - that is a process of dissipation. If our concept of absolute entropy is correct - galaxies should be shrinking rather than growing. Though there may be some that are shrinking, there may be some that are disintegrating, but the evidence is that the overwhelming majority of galaxies are growing. How does this fit in with our belief that the cosmos is running down - following the entrenched error that it all commenced billions of earth years ago in some hypothetical primeval nuclear explosion? Observations of galactic growth do not fit in with the theories of academic cosmologists. Something has to give. So far there has been little sign that cosmologists understand the cosmos beyond realising that humanity, having released nuclear energy, now believe that this must be the core of reality. But little more than a century ago the Sun itself was conceived as though it were a mass of burning coal! Are we really any wiser now with our concept of nuclear energy being the prime cosmic reality? It is Reich's work that has opened a door - a door that has been ignored - rather than investigated.

Nuclear energy

But supposing you still continue to uphold the concept that entropy is the end result of everything and that all is destined to dissolve into dead energy no longer of any use to neither man nor beast. Then we have to concede that energy is prime to matter. Given that reasoning, nuclear structure therefore must be secondary to energy and not the prime basis of reality. But how did it all come about?

Nuclear energy is dispersive - what is left after nuclear explosion is not a plethora of valuable heavy elements and metals but a vast amount of wounded matter in dangerously radioactive states; states that only pollute and are antithetical to creation. Is it at all likely that in those wounded remnants following nuclear disintegration we will find the ultimate secret of the cosmos? How then can the concept of the 'big bang' still have any credibility? Following this line of reasoning how can nuclear physics ever hope to penetrate to primary cosmic law?

Evidence of growth rather than decay in the cosmos

Recent astronomical research has brought to light the remarkable fact that galaxies themselves tend to cluster together and in many cases material intergalactic bridges have formed between adjacent galaxies. So ubiquitous are these phenomena that Palomar Observatory astronomer Fritz Zwicky expressed the opinion that such intergalactic bridges may be the rule rather than the exception. These bridges appear similar in nature to galactic spiral arms; that is, young Population One[8] stars and associated nebulae and 'dust'.

So now we have unequivocal evidence for clusters of galaxies and a strong indication of material growth i.e. the intergalactic bridges. As a consequence cosmic growth must be vast enough to include all these clusters of galaxies or metagalaxies. Following our previous reasoning, in order to maintain the concept of absolute entropy, we must postulate a force even greater than a metagalaxy. Clearly the evidence today contradicts the postulate that entropy is absolute. By realising that entropy is but one cosmic function amongst others the contradiction between observation and theory can be resolved.

Reconsidering the phenomenon of growth

To recapitulate, we have seen how the phenomenon of growth operates on all cosmic levels. The proponents of the absolute law of thermodynamics (entropy) dismiss the phenomena of growth as contradictory to entropy as growth seemingly is dependent upon the next higher cosmic level. Just as it is averred, that life, although a growth phenomena, could not exist without the solar radiation - radiation that is viewed as entropy. But realising that growth is a universal phenomenon, not limited to life on earth alone but is universal - the only way we can maintain the concept of absolute entropy is by postulating a force greater than anything we know (with or without instrumentation). Cosmologists deductive reasoning has become a cul de sac of supposition that is neither proved or disproved.

The law of entropy applies only to a secondary realm of nature. Cosmic Metabolism does not deny entropy but understands that it is only one aspect of the cosmos. It also shows that energetic functions are prime to material functions. We need to perceive energetic functions as a unity or totality before we can understand creation on any cosmic level, whether terrestrial or galactic. Mechanistic science has delved deeper and deeper into the microcosm, failing to realise that no matter how much we learn about a building brick it tells us little about the building itself.

At this point I find it necessary to give a brief synopsis of psychoanalytic and depth psychological discoveries and how these led to the breakthrough into the physical realm. It is regrettable that these discoveries are not better known; if they were the following explanation would be unnecessary. These are not meant to replace first hand study, but merely to acquaint and I hope stimulate the interest to study. Also they help to make comprehensible my viewpoint and my realisations in cosmology.

---

[8] Astronomers class stars into two divisions – young stars are classified as Population One and Population Two are old stars.

2. A four-beat life cycle; tension, charge, discharge and relaxation[9].

Depth psychology[10]

My acquaintance with depth psychology happened seemingly by chance. As a very dissatisfied young man, I spent three years (1946-1949) attempting to understand philosophy, in a search to comprehend myself and the world about me. I felt much loneliness and longing during that time. Believing myself unattractive to women and frequently feeling painfully shy, I attempted to acquire intellectual ability with the hope that by so doing I could win fame and a beautiful woman.

It was many years before I finally realised that attractiveness isn't a matter of genes, but of aliveness. Not finding the hoped for answer in philosophy, I kept searching and during the latter part of this period, reviving a childhood interest in the stars, I read many books about astronomy.

Having also studied as a musician, in 1949, I took employment as a jazz musician on the transatlantic liner "Queen Mary" and during a voyage a fellow musician loaned me a book about Freud's discoveries, which impressed me strongly. In retrospect I don't know how much I really learned at that time, but I was very impressed with the concept of the unconscious and that much of our motivation stems from deeper levels than that of consciousness. I believe the realisation that sexuality is a biological force (a fact I had never before considered) may have helped to relieve me of some of the guilt and anxiety that I felt so strongly at times.

My next contact with psychoanalytic writings happened as a result of a conversation with the noted jazz musician Lennie Tristano. Having learned that Lennie was interested in Freud's concepts, I mentioned that I had read a book about Freud. Lennie's answer - an answer I have never forgotten was "If you want to know about Bird's (Charlie Parker's) music - you don't listen to his imitators to find out - you listen to Bird himself". In other words, go to the source, and the same with Freud - he made the discoveries - find out what he said from his own writings. Many times that has come back to me "If you want to find out, go to the source."

Subsequently I read every book of Freud's that I could get. Some time later - I believe early in 1952 - another musician friend, drummer Jeff Morton, loaned me a copy of Wilhelm Reich's The Function of the Orgasm. At first I was half hearted about reading it, but as I got into the book the force of the writing literally compelled me to read it. I soon realised that although comparatively unknown here were discoveries and realisations of major importance.

As a direct result of reading this book, I underwent psychotherapy and

---

[9] While this next section was summarised in Chapter 1, I have left it in this extract because it is integral to the argument.

[10] Depth psychology is a term that refers to disciplines such as psychoanalysis while psychology is a generic term in the literature.

spent the next six years re-learning emotionally what I had already coldly learned intellectually. The decade from 1952 to 1961 was for me a stormy period of much emotional upheaval and many disappointments, but it seems to have led me to a kind of emancipation; less of sublimation of instinctual drives and more of direct expression of them.

Reich's concept of orgone - physical life energy

Unfortunately Dr. Reich's discoveries, though almost totally ignored by the world at large, quickly became a cult, especially amongst many musicians and artists, and though through the experience of psychotherapy I had developed a real appreciation of his character analytic discoveries, I was initially thrown into doubt in regard to his concept of the physical life energy (orgone).

Many people accepted uncritically the concept and findings of Orgonomy (the study of the life energy) - seeming to do so without true seriousness - thus making it appear as though merely a fad or a cult; whilst others unhesitatingly ridiculed the entire concept. Very few have given Reich's findings the serious attention they deserve.

I built an Orgone accumulator for myself; used it, thought I believed, but then time and time again I would be thrown into doubt, by criticism or ridicule by others. Sometimes I would demonstrate my accumulator; inviting sceptics to find out for themselves. Frequently, after ten or fifteen minutes they would begin to get red in the face and more often than not they would become angry and say to me vehemently, "It's a hoax, I don't feel a thing. Gee it's hot in here what are you trying to do to me anyway?"

I finally learned not to demonstrate. Most of this, I now believe, was due mainly to my own insecurity and indecision, Gradually I learned to depend more upon my own observations and though still learning from others observations, I am now far less dependent upon their approval.

To gain some understanding of how Orgonomic discoveries evolved, we must go back to the early 1920's during the time Reich was a member physician in the Vienna Psychoanalytic Society. Freud's discoveries of the sexual etiology of neurosis, is a well proven, if not yet widely accepted fact. However his concept of instinctual energy, the so-called libido - without which the neurotic symptom remains unintelligible - remains undeveloped in psychoanalysis even to this day.

Before Freud the term libido meant the feeling or desire (for sexual activity). Freud had stated that we do not feel the instinct as such, but only it's derivatives, sexual ideas and feelings. The instinct is biological and makes itself felt as an urge for release of tension.

Reich's interpretation of this was that it is logical that the instinct cannot be conscious, for it governs us. As in electrical phenomena, we do not know what it is, we only realise its manifestations such as light and shock.

Though the electric manifestation is measurable, we are merely measuring a manifestation of electricity. And just as we measure electricity through its manifestations so we recognise instincts through emotional manifestations. Reich continued, it may eventually become possible to measure libido, and he used the analogy of electricity without suspecting that sixteen years later he would be able to demonstrate the identity of sexual and bioelectrical energetic manifestations.

Therapeutic work with neurotics convinced Reich that genital disturbance is the prime symptom of neurosis. This concept met much criticism from Reich's colleagues, and resulted in his examining his findings even more thoroughly than before. In the course of two years he had collected enough evidence to conclude that genital disturbance is not merely one symptom amongst others, but it is THE symptom of neurosis.

It then became clear that neurosis is not merely a sexual disturbance (as Freud had formulated) but is the result of a genital disturbance - orgastic impotence. If Reich had restricted the concept of sexuality to that of genitality, he would have been reverting to the erroneous concept of sexuality before Freud. Instead, by extending the concept of genital functioning to the realisation that the neurosis is a result of genital disturbance (or orgastic impotence) further psychoanalytic insight was gained.

The blocking of bio-sexual energy

Thorough investigation and work with neurotic patients revealed the following facts.

Every neurotic disturbance has a core of damned up bio-sexual energy. The source of the neurosis lies in the differential between accumulation and discharge of such energy.

Freud's therapeutic formula, of bringing the repressed sexuality to consciousness, is incomplete. The first therapeutic task is, indeed, to make repressed sexuality conscious. Though this may result in cure, it does not necessarily do so. Health is re-established only if the source of energy, the sexual stasis is also eliminated. The goal of therapy then becomes the establishment of orgastic potency.

Reich further realised that elucidation of the neurotic symptom led to analysis of the entire personality and that what characterised the symptom (as distinct from the less obvious aspects of neuroses) was the fact that the patient invariably felt the symptom as alien to him, whereas the subtler aspects of the neurotic syndrome are usually thoroughly rationalised. Gradually it became clear that a successful analysis entailed analysis of the entire personality.

Character Analysis

A basic dynamic factor is that the patient resists the analysis by all possible means and constantly defends himself against facing that within himself that is neurotic. Ultimately this resolves in defences against genitality. This defensive resistance is complicated by the fact that it is usually hidden (frequently by an apparently positive transference[11]).

In his book "Character Analysis", Reich gives examples from case histories, demonstrating the importance of bringing the hidden negative transference to the fore. Until this is achieved no real progress can be made. If the negative transference is neglected, and if as often happens, it remains hidden under an apparent positive transference; the chaotic situation may result and the patient's intellectual awareness then has little or no effect upon his actual neurotic condition. In such cases the intellectual awareness bounces back from a wall of repressed hatred (the latent negative transference).

Awareness of those dynamic factors, and development of a technique that concentrated on bringing the latent negative transference to the fore, of necessity, tackles both emotional and psychic aspects. Reich termed this method Character Analysis.

Armouring - Physical as well as psychoanalysis techniques are needed

The next major discovery in the elucidation of neurosis was the realisation that the energy stasis (the energetic source of the neurosis) is bound in the musculature. The neurosis manifests in the psychic realm as neurotic symptoms and character attitudes, and in the somatic realm as muscular tension and biological rigidity.

Henceforth the breaking down of the neurosis no longer depended wholly upon psychoanalytic techniques, but could also be apprehended somatically (i.e. the body as distinct from the mind). Reich found that the energy was bound in muscles in segmental groups, transverse to the torso and these groups do not correspond to the muscle nerve groups of classical biology.

Biological rigidity resulting from the energy bound within these segmental groups Reich described as muscular armouring. The armouring has the function of reducing the flow of biological energy, thus holding the painful neurotic symptoms to a minimum.

Expansion and Contraction - the life cycle

Further investigation established that what is perceived psychically as anxiety is manifested somatically as biological contraction and what is perceived as pleasure is somatically identical to biological expansion.

---

[11] Transference is a term used in psychoanalysis to describe a patient's attachment to the therapist, as though the therapist is a substitute father or mother figure.

Individual organs and living organisms as a whole, function in pulsation between expansion and contraction. Reich defined a four-beat life cycle; tension, charge, discharge and relaxation. The phenomena of tension and charge are accompanied by expansion of the organism, while the discharge and subsequent relaxation take place through orgastic convulsion. This is the basic function of all life processes governing, not only the orgastic function, but also cell division, respiration, heartbeat, peristalsis etc.

In attempts to discover the nature of life energy Reich examined cooked foodstuff. High power microscopic examination revealed that cooked food, whether fat, starch or protein - breaks down into tiny vesicles that refract light strongly. If allowed to develop these vesicles will, after a period of days, clump together and eventually form protozoa. Thus spontaneously, new life evolves.

These vesicles, Reich termed 'bions' and they will form from a multitude of substances in addition to food. The main prerequisite seems to be heating - though in the case of organic material such as food, heating appears inessential - but it does accelerate the process. Reich succeeded in cultivating bions from such substances as bituminous coal, blood charcoal, iron filings, ocean sand, earth etc. The bions are intermediate forms between non-life and life. This discovery subsequently led to an understanding of the cancer disease.

Understanding cancer

Protozoa develop from bionously disintegrating moss and grass tissue and, from suffocating bionously disintegrating human and animal tissue, develops the cancer cell. The cancer cell is the "protozoa" of dying animal tissue. The carcinomatous tumour is an end product of dying animal tissue and is a result and not the cause of the cancer disease. The fact that advanced cancer patients are invariably resigned, emotionally dead individuals, also bears out this concept of cancer as a slow dying.

In experimental physical orgone therapy Reich discovered that provided tumour growth hadn't proceeded beyond a certain limit, the tumours could be naturally eliminated, and the patient apparently regained health. However if the tumours had grown beyond a certain limit, recharging the organism through use of the orgone accumulator, often resulted in tumour dissolution, but invariably death occurred, through secondary disorders of liver, kidney or lymph glands.

The recharging of the organism reversed the dying process and resulted in the disintegration of tumours, but tumours beyond a certain size, proved too much of a burden upon the organs of elimination and purification and death resulted. Cancer patients in whom tumours hadn't developed to this critical stage, apparently recovered, but in many cases shortly after apparent cure a severe neurosis manifested.

Breathing - blocking unpleasant emotions but also blocking energy

Subsequent therapy revealed that the neurosis had developed long before the onset of the cancer disease itself and cancer had appeared following characterological resignation from apparently insoluble neurotic tensions in life situations. Cancer can then be recognised primarily as a sex or love starvation disease[12].

Some time earlier, Reich had realised that faulty breathing (particularly - holding the breath) is the prime mechanism of inhibiting unpleasant emotions. At first this may be done consciously, but after a while the ability to breathe naturally may be entirely lost. Inability to breathe naturally is characteristic of all neurotic conditions, and as holding the breath inhibits the flow of biological energy, it results in a damming up of the energy and thus leads to formation of armouring. The armouring of the breathing function, Reich termed 'respiratory block' and it is found in varying degrees in all neuroses and biopathic disease, (that is disease resulting from bio-psychic conflicts).

Before closing this chapter, I will again repeat, that this synopsis of Reich's work is not meant to replace Reich's writings, but is intended to stimulate interest - to encourage you to read for yourselves from the source - this great discovery.

Summing up his work (in the last paragraph of "The Function of the Orgasm") Reich states how the investigation of living matter has proceeded beyond depth psychology and physiology, and has now entered previously unexplored territory. A new road into the problem of biogenesis has now been opened. Psychology has led to biophysics but its core remains always the same, "the enigma of love to which we owe our being."

3 The Orgone Accumulator

Experiments with bions - energy vesicles and the energy they produce

Among the many successful bion preparations made, one type that was developed from ocean sand, named SAPA bions (SAnd PAcket) in Reich's research are especially strong biologically. Reich found that these SAPA bions kill or paralyse cancer cells even at a distance of ten microns. A strong skin reaction was observed when a SAPA culture was brought in close contact with the skin for ten minutes (but separated by the quartz slide). Reich's eyes began to hurt when he looked at these cultures under the microscope for too long a time.

Using a monocular microscope and observing with one eye only, limited the irritation to the eye being used. Reich stated that he eventually

---

[12] This does not take into account the enormous increase in cancer in recent years. It is clear that environmental factors, chemical and radiation pollution are now also significant factors in modern disease patterns.

developed a severe conjunctivitis that necessitated relinquishing microscopic work for some time. After treatment the eye improved, but now he knew he was dealing with a radiation. Gradually he realised that the air in the room containing the cultures became "heavy" and many people developed headaches if the windows remained closed for an hour or so. Metal objects became magnetised and photographic plates left in the room with the cultures became fogged.

While working in the dark room containing the cultures (after adapting to the darkness) Reich became aware that the room appeared grey-blue and not black. There were fog-like phenomena and bluish lines of light. The impressions became stronger and larger through a magnifying glass.

Rubber gloves, paper, cotton, cellulose and other organic substances left in close proximity with the cultures, produce strong deflection of the electroscope. High humidity, ventilation and touching of the objects with the hands, reduce or eliminate the reaction.

An enclosure was designed for the purpose of containing the energy radiated by the cultures. From working with the electroscope Reich deduced that what was needed was a box made of wood or other organic material and lined with sheet metal. A lens was put in the front wall, through which the luminating energy could be viewed from the outside. The result was successful. It was possible to observe bluish moving vapours and light, yellowish points and lines. This was confirmed by several observers.

But then, incomprehensibly, when the cultures were removed from the box, the radiation phenomena were still there, although of lesser intensity.

Orgone - basic life energy

Reich had another box built, but without the organic material and kept carefully away from the SAPA cultures, but still the phenomena appeared. After a great deal of bewilderment and subsequent experimentation, he finally realised that the energy is present everywhere, but in varying concentration.

Further observation led to the inescapable conclusion that there is an energy present in the atmosphere that is identical to our body energy. It is stronger around life systems; humans, animals and plants; stronger on clear sunny days, than on cloudy or humid days and weakest shortly before and during rain. It can be seen as a bluish flickering and moving points of light in the orgone energy darkroom, also between the stars on a clear dark night. It can also be observed in clouds at night and around plants (particularly flowers) at night. During the day, by looking into the blue sky - into the distance - it can be seen as luminous, whitish spiralling points and vapourous sheets that pulsate across the sky.

This energy that is present everywhere, Reich termed Orgone. from the words organism and orgasm. From these observations and from the energetic flow within organisms, the basic life energetic movement was discovered - that of the spinning wave or "kreiselwelle".

Orgone energy's spiral movement

The basic animal and plant form, the orgonome is a result of the spiralling movement confined within a membrane. In genitality, two organisms superimpose. The function of the genital embrace can only be fully understood through comprehension of the fact that two orgone energy systems (organisms) experience mutual attraction, lumination and then merge; finally experiencing complete orgastic surrender and becoming energetically one. Functionally identical is the orgone energy darkroom phenomena of two spiralling luminating energetic points, coming together and merging in a tiny spark of light. This is the basis of creation, whether it be the formation of new life or seed; growth of a planet or sun or creative thinking or action.

Reich's concept of the functional identity of hurricane, sunspot and galactic formation, proceeds from the discoveries of orgone energy physics and he viewed the spiralling movements of galaxies, planets, sunspots and hurricanes as cosmic manifestations of orgonomic law.

Orgone Energy Accumulator

It is from this starting point that my own investigations of what has been discovered by orthodox astronomy began. The first orgone energy accumulator was the box built to house the SAPA cultures. But it took a great deal of further experimentation by Reich to establish that such a device will accumulate orgone energy from the surrounding energy field even in the absence of SAPA or other bionous cultures.

This natural function takes place as follows. Organic or non metallic mineral matter attracts and holds orgone energy. Conversely metallic matter, while initially attracting orgone energy repels it again. A box built of organic or non metallic mineral matter and lined with sheet metal will naturally accumulate orgone energy. The non-metallic components attract the energy, while the metal lining attracts and then repels the energy. The net result being that some of the energy attracted by the metal is reflected back to the non-metallic material and the rest is absorbed and then reflected to the inside. The result is a higher potential within the enclosure. Increasing the number of layers, alternate non-metal and metal, increases the potential within the enclosure.

Many manufactured devices - made for purposes other than orgone accumulation, nevertheless function as accumulators. In electrical circuitry - condensers, resistors, transformers all modify the surrounding energy - regardless of whether in use or not. Clearly when in use the surrounding energy is modified even further[13]. Other orgone energy discoveries

---

[13] One of the main effects upon what today is ubiquitously referred to as global warming is the modification of the atmospheric orgone energy as a result of the increased use of electricity and electronics.

proceed from the observation that water soaks up orgone energy. That water is the prime cleanser can further be understood from this standpoint of cosmic energy.

As Reich discovered, metal draws and then immediately repels orgone energy. It then follows that when one end of a metal pipe is placed in water the water draws the energy from the pipe and the interior of the pipe is depleted of energy. This sets up a drawing action and the pipe then draws energy from the surrounding atmosphere. A series of pipes placed parallel to one another will create a strong drawing action – withdrawing energy from a room or from a person close by. This helps to remove the stagnant energy of that person and thus helps to eliminate the tendency to disease.

A large group of metal pipes, when placed in water, can similarly affect the atmosphere. and as such can help to modify weather. Reich used such devices to create rain in drought stricken areas, and in the last months before his work was curtailed, he succeeded in modifying the weather in the Arizona desert to the extent that prairie grass began to grow – where it had never previously been known. This last series of experiments heralded a scientific potential that was cut short by the infamous Food and Drug Administration's injunction that prevented the continuation of his research.

The fact that accumulating devices just described create higher potentials than the surrounding atmosphere, are prime examples of reversal of entropy, thus proving that current concepts of entropy are false. As previously pointed out these facts invalidate the absolute interpretation of the second law of thermodynamics.

Another major discovery in Orgone physics is presented in his book "The Oranur Experiment". If orgone energy concentrations are irritated beyond a certain level, the energy itself changes its nature and then manifests certain deadly qualities. The energy becomes stagnant and stale and can seriously disturb life functions. Such changes from benign to deadly energy resulted from experiments that subjected concentrated orgone energy fields to irritation by electromagnetic and nuclear energy. The orgone energy reacts as though to fight the deadly influence and in so doing, if irritated beyond certain levels, it changes and itself becomes a killer energy. Reich termed this changed energy DOR (Deadly Orgone). Attempts to clear the atmosphere of the noxious DOR energy led to the development of the cloud buster.

Reich's discoveries

As a final reference, a summary of the body of work and Reich's fundamental discoveries illustrates his contribution to scientific knowledge:

1/ The orgasm theory and the development of the technique of Character

Analysis.

2/ Discovery of muscular armouring and the respiratory block.

3/ Concept of sex-economic self regulation of primary natural drives as distinct from secondary perverted drives.

4/ The role of irrationalism and human sex-economy in the origin of dictatorship

5/ Discovery of the energy function of the orgasm reflex.

6/ The bioelectrical nature of sexuality, and of pleasure and anxiety.

7/ Discovery of bions - orgone energy vesicles

8/ Origin of the cancer cell from bionously disintegrating animal tissue and the functionally identical organisation of protozoa from bionously disintegrating moss and grass tissue.

9/ Discovery of T-bacilli; discovery of the Orgone energy in SAPA bions

10/ Discovery of the atmospheric Orgone energy.

11/ Invention of the Orgone accumulator.

12/ Experimental Orgone therapy of the cancer disease.

13/ Investigation of biogenesis

14/ Orgonomic functionalism

15/ The Orgonotic Geiger Action

16/ Discovery of a motor force in Orgone energy.

17/ The concept of the emotional plague as a disease of bioenergetic disequilibrium.

18/ Concept of Cosmic Superimposition.

19/ Oranur - Orgone against Nuclear energy

20/ DOR deadly orgone.

21/ Foundation of pre-atomic chemistry.

22/ The cloudbuster and weather control.

23/ Theory of desert formation - in nature and in man.

24/ Demonstration of reversibility of desert formation.

25/ Theory of disease - based upon biological accumulation of DOR energy

26/ Gravity and antigravity equations.

Section 3

Extract 1979: Cosmic Metabolism and Cosmic Energy

Feeling Like A Lone Voice

Chapter 5 - Cosmic Metabolism and Cosmic Energy[14]
Dissipative as well as Expansive Properties of Energy

"There are no experts in the realm of new knowledge."
                                              Wilhelm Reich

The universal flow - the endless movement of energy

Cosmic Metabolism is a new paradigm in cosmic understanding. It is a scientific analysis of the universal flow. There is an endless movement of energy that radiates into space, which of course is well known. What is not taken into account is that such radiation eventually reaches an extreme tenuosity upon which it becomes condensative, eventually forming new matter. This is the ultimate creative cycle. The energy released from material breakdown is dissipative. Only in reaching deep space does this transformation occur. It is this transformation that science has not yet recognised. Cosmic flow processes are analogous to those of a liquid and can be thought of as endless distillation. Whereas liquids need a container to hold them and distillation processes need apparatus to contain them, the cosmos is not a container; it is an endless (literally endless) plexus of open flow patterns.

What we recognise as "matter" is merely one point (a kind of stopover) in this endless process. Energies condense into matter, but matter is not a permanent state. Matter eventually breaks down and the energy flows onward and outward into space once more. This is the true meaning of relativity. There is infinity not only of space, but also of time. This 'container less' reality functions entirely according to laws of affinity and repulsion. Our preoccupation with boundaries to space and time comes about through our being part of a culture that is overwhelmingly materialistic and possessive.

The qualities of cosmic energy

Cosmic energies manifest different qualities or laws of function, according to the place they occupy in the cosmic cycle. These qualities (which I shall describe in some detail) are themselves not absolute, but are merely aspects pertaining to the overall pattern of dissolution, material formation and material breakdown - an endless cyclic flow. This cyclic process manifests as a duality that is expressed as energy before matter (condensative, creative, centripetal flow) and energy after matter (evaporative, dissipative, entropic flow). The cosmos is not a reality created at some moment in the past (the mythical 'big bang'), nor is it destined to cease at some time in the future (the supposed 'heat death'[15] scenario).

---

[14] As described in Chapter 3, this extract is from my writing in 1979. Again additional headings, minor changes and explanatory footnotes have been added.

[15] Discussed in Chapter 4.

Orthodox science is unduly preoccupied with materialism and particularly with the exploitation of energies derived from matter. As a result, only one aspect of the cosmic duality has been taken into account and this pertains to material functioning and of the potential energy it contains. The word energy is used indiscriminately. We talk about energy contained within fossil fuels; we talk of nuclear energy; when we have a good day we might say we are feeling energetic. The word "energy" is also regarded as a kind of potential. We talk of latent energy. Energy locked up within a molecule, or nuclear energy locked up within matter, or of life energy. The fact that nuclear energy and life energy are different extremes of the cosmic cycle, is unrecognised by orthodox science, and as a result totally ignored.

The cosmic duality - condensative and dissipative energy

With a scientific viewpoint that is limited to one aspect of the cosmic duality, it is impossible to gain a true picture of cosmic functions. Whereas the energy processes that science deals with are dissipative and entropic - to postulate that all energy processes are - ipso facto - subject to the same laws is a great error. This error underlies all orthodox scientific thinking (including current views on cosmology) and there can be no real progress in understanding cosmology while this error is perpetuated.

Prime condensative energy does not travel at the speed of light, neither is its movement linear. It is slow moving and if unimpeded flows in a spinning wave - the kreiselwelle. Its tendency or 'cosmic direction' is condensative. The open spinning wave contracts, becoming subject to the influence of surrounding matter. This is the genesis of gravitation (which is an ongoing process) and the kreiselwelle movement is transformed to one of vortical condensation and a particle is born. It is paradoxical, but supremely logical, that an increase in the rate of spin goes hand in hand with the slowing down and eventual cessation of spatial movement. The aesthetic beauty of a ballet dancer increasing spin by pulling the arms close to the body mirrors this reality. The laws of angular momentum have their genesis here.

Vortical processes [the spiralling movement of energy] occur on every level throughout the cosmos. In the microcosmos - observing live vorticellae in pond water - we can see the organic detritus that constitute their food are sucked in by a whirlpool movement. White blood cells paralyse alien bacteria and as this occurs the invading bacteria commence spinning - a movement that marks their death throes as individual living units. Turning to the macrocosmic arena, a meteor or satellite increases its rate of spin as it enters the earth's atmosphere. Clouds - being condensative phenomena also manifest spin - which is particularly obvious in time lapse photography. None of these processes take place at the speed of light. Nor is the movement linear, but vortical. Taking examples from such different levels of reality is not an undisciplined use of analogy, but demonstrate that such processes are aspects of universal law.

Wilhelm Reich was the first to bring attention to what he rightly termed 'functional identity' in the entire realm of nature - from micro to macrocosmos. Using the term 'orgone' from organism and orgasm, he focussed the concept of life energy - beyond the somewhat vague or mystical - and showed how this is indeed the universal energy. Though the Newtonian conception of gravity and repetition of the apparent planetary movement is useful for our concepts of time i.e. the clockwork model of the universe, the Cartesian view of cosmic vortexes, when developed further will enable us to understand energy processes in a more fundamental way, than the current limitation of using the expansive principle of fire as though it were the sole energy.

The very structure of living organisms, reflects the vortical nature of their energy. Energy that is confined within a membrane. Peristaltic movement, heartbeat and blood flow through arteries and veins, indicate the existence of an energy that is pulsatory as regards time and vortical as regards spatial movement. None of this can be understood from the vantage point of electromagnetic theory or from concepts that stem from the belief in absolute entropy - concepts that apply solely to the secondary aspect of cosmic functioning - that of energy from matter. Orthodox cosmology has considered the living as though it were merely some kind of cosmic accident that can at best maintain a tenuous hold in those rare areas of space that by chance are not too hot or too cold. Orthodoxy believes the cosmos to be running down and consequently life must count for very little in such a universe of decay.

Energy as the basic creative force - matter from energy

The reality is however very different. Life is an aspect of the formative energy and this energy is the basic creative force. The movement of planets, stars and star clusters is also vortical. Galaxies also reflect this vortical movement as is evidenced by their structure. Closer to home, sunspots have a spiral structure and the entire solar photosphere manifests turbulence, that is an interaction between prime vorticity and radiation. Hurricanes and tornadoes are also a vortical manifestation and planetary weather is a turbulent vorticity - likewise an interaction between the vortical (condensative) and radiative (dissipative) energies. None of these cosmic energy movements are' 'contained'. Neither were they set in motion at some time in the remote past in some mysterious way.

The vortical movements are natural energy actions that are superior as a power source, far superior to our attempts to harness the dissipative energy of fossil fuels or by nuclear breakdown. But before we can harness this prime energy force, we must of course first learn to recognise its existence.

Energy from matter - fire/ fossil fuel energy

Having sketched a picture, conceptualising the two forces that are actually two poles of an underlying unity, let us take a closer look at the secondary pole of cosmic functioning, that of energy from matter. As is now realised, matter is frozen energy. This is fine in theory, though as yet , even with nuclear breakdown we can unlock only a small amount of the energy of which matter is composed. Until a half century ago we could only tap the energy locked within the outer layers of matter - those pertaining to molecular structure. And it is that energy released from the catalytic breakdown of fossil fuels that even to this day remains the main source of power upon which we have come to depend, i.e. the energy of fire. The qualities of fire energy are expansiveness and heat, and it is the expansive principle that powers the steam engine, the piston engine, the jet turbine and the rocket.

The principle behind both heat and expansiveness is that of dissipation. The steam engine was of course the first discovery of how this energy could be harnessed. Then for the first time in recorded history we had at our command a source of energy independent of human or animal muscle power. True there had been some previous use of wind or water power, but the steam engine was the first machine to use the expansive principle latent in combustion. And just at that time came the first conceptual error. The awe of witnessing a machine generating its own power led to the false presumption that humanity had solved the secret of cosmic power. In fact only now, two hundred years later are we emerging from misconceiving life as though it were merely an elaborate machine that functions on a kind of chemical fire energy. From such misconceptions came the errors of today's cosmological thinking. The wonder of watching a powerful machine (which still fascinates every child) gradually led to the mistaken view that the secrets of cosmic power were finally revealed, through harnessing fire energy. When in the mid nineteen forties America developed the atom bomb, the shift in emphasis - was "now the secret of the universe has been revealed".

A culture that knows more and more about less and less

There is a strong sociological factor that also plays a part in such misconceptions that have developed in cosmology. Isaac Newton - a great innovator - developed many new concepts. Best remembered for his concept of gravitation, he also developed, together with Leibnitz, the mathematical concepts of logarithms (which he called fluxions) and his concept of light as corpuscular phenomena became a founding concept of our understanding of light. A practical man, he designed and built his own reflecting telescope - a type still known as the Newtonian Reflector. Such men as Newton are the intellectual giants of humanity. It is understandable that such men are revered long after their time. Our institute of learning regard such men as icons whose work every undergraduate has to assimilate. Rightly so, but this spawns another problem - that of stifling original thought.

The twentieth century came under the influence of Einstein in a similar way. I remember vividly a conversation I had in 1973 with Dr. Charles Whitney, then professor of astronomy at Harvard University. We had what became a somewhat heated discussion about current cosmological thinking, which he admitted was far from satisfactory. I had pointed out that there were certain irrationalities about Einstein's concept of relativity (which indeed Einstein himself was less than satisfied with). According to Professor Whitney, the problem in presenting new cosmological concepts was, in his words " you can't counter Einstein". Such attitudes infect virtually all intellectual professions. It is well known that to write an acceptable PhD thesis, the concern is more with the acknowledgement of existing published sources rather than original thought. Valid or not - original thought - can lead to rejection of the thesis. The effect of this is to breed generations of very bright scholars, in whom any germ of originality has been stifled. When in turn they become the professors who mentor later generations, they perpetuate this culture of conformity. This is a prime reason why we have developed a culture that knows more and more about less and less.

There are times when we need to take a fresh look and start again. Indeed this is what Freud did in his early days, and that was the legacy Reich inherited. Reich, whom later generations may come to realise as possibly the greatest scientist of the twentieth century, was pilloried throughout his life, because he investigated sexuality, without subscribing to the prurient attitudes of society as a whole. Finally his discoveries were dismissed as fraud. We know the outcome. His books were burned; he was jailed by the US authorities and died there.

As I pointed out it is little more than a century ago when the sun's lifespan was estimated as though it were composed of burning coal. By extrapolation, other stars were believed to be similarly burning away. The recurring aspects of apparent stellar and planetary movement, upon which terrestrial clocks were synchronised, led to a cosmological model of clockwork and fire. Both of these aspects were of course entropic. It is the second law of thermodynamics, which states that energy potential always changes from high to low and that energy cannot of itself pass from low to high. That is invalid on the cosmic level[16]. From this fallacious concept comes the view that the universe is running down, and eventually there will be an even potential of energy everywhere; the so called "heat death". Though the entropy law (the second law of thermodynamics discussed already) is valid for the mechanical realm, it is obvious that it is not valid in the realm of the living. Life has higher energy levels than the environment. This awkward fact is overlooked by mechanistic science. It has also contributed to the belief that life is some kind of cosmic accident that could not maintain itself, were it not for the Sun's energy - that of

---

[16] As discussed in the previous chapter

course is believed to be dissipating and entirely subject to the laws of entropy.

So life, viewed as some kind of cosmic accident, is secondary to the current view of the cosmos, a cosmos that according to cosmologists had some beginning in time, when all matter was created in a massive 'big bang' and has since been expanding into the cosmos of today. In this view the second law of thermodynamics reigns supreme, notwithstanding that life does not function according to this law, nor does the cosmos where new stars are actively being born. Of course the birth of new stars can conveniently be explained as parts of the cosmos that failed to ignite completely in that mythical instant of the big bang! The late starters in the rush to the heat death! Within this orthodox but mistaken view of cosmic reality, "time" is also a finite phenomenon and the limitations and inconsistencies of this cosmic model, have led to much wild theorising in attempts to break out from such restrictive concepts.

Indeed despite their intricacies, today's cosmologies are merely sophisticated elaborations of the naïve eighteenth and nineteenth century speculations. In fact many of today's cosmological complexities stem (not so much from the vast amount of data gathered - which by rights should give us a clearer understanding) but from trying to fit current findings into a basically faulty model. It is as though we are busy trying to find edge pieces to a gigantic jigsaw puzzle, when in fact there are no edge pieces to infinity. The cosmos is a containerless reality functioning according to the laws of attraction and repulsion. It is orthodox theory that insists upon boxing it in with concepts of absolute genesis and final cessation. Future cultures will no doubt look upon such views as childishly naïve.

In the early part of the twentieth century estimates of the "lifespan" of the cosmos were drastically extended. Through revision of ideas concerning the cause of stellar lumination (no longer conceived as chemical combustion, but nuclear fission) the original picture of the cosmos created at some remote past and thenceforth subject to gradual dissipation has remained unchanged. Only the postulated date of creation was extended further back into the past and the postulated heat death further forward into the future.

Entropy is not an end process - growth after the dissipation of energy

Neither is this denying the reality of entropy. Entropy is not an end process as is currently believed, but is a function. Its function is to transform. Webster's Dictionary describes entropy as "the theoretical measure of energy, as of steam, which cannot be transformed into work in a thermodynamic system". However this is not a cosmic description, but a value judgement. The error here is of judging entropic processes as having no further place or function in the cosmos once they have dissipated to a point whereby they are no longer of use to us. As previously pointed out, entropic processes eventually reach a point that even stellar energy no longer poses a hazard to life once it has dissipated sufficiently into deep space. But in dissipating it is transformed. For once such energy has dissipated to the point where it can safely be assimilated by the living, as is the case with solar energy reaching us here on earth, it becomes essential to the well being of life on earth. Life is part of the condensative, creative pole of reality, and the entropic energy radiated from the sun has transformed by its journey through space into condensative energy - now absorbed by the planet and by the living. The changes that we have taken for granted as quantitative - that is entropy - which we have judged to be an end process are actually qualitative changes and are the clues to understanding the missing link in cosmology.

The principle also applies to nuclear radiation as released here on earth. Unlike say a wood fire, which is comparatively benign, energy released from the atomic nucleus, needs not only much time to neutralise (as is well known and described as the 'half life') but also vast distances in which to dissipate. The artificial release of nuclear radiation (whether from the nuclear reactors or from a nuclear fireball) is incredibly expansive and dissipative. Having been trapped within the atomic nucleus, when released it passes straight through any matter that stands in its way. In so doing it creates havoc on the matter through which it passes. The phenomena of what is called secondary radiation is indicative of the damage caused by primary radiation. The chemistry of the affected matter is drastically changed as elemental nuclei are transformed into other elements. When life is exposed to such (gamma) radiation, the body chemistry is drastically altered. The biological molecular structure alters and continues to change as the bioplasm tries to adjust and repair the radiation damage. Nuclear radiation is a stellar function and creating such reactions on earth profoundly disturb the biosphere. Even if we ignore the physical damage to life's chemistry, the energy effect is also disastrous as Reich's Oranur experimentation[17] clearly showed. The creation of what is in effect, stellar energy on Earth, is one of the main reasons for the disruption we call global warming, or climate change. This artificial nuclear disruption, hinders what would be normal metabolism of pollutants. Added to this the huge increase of chemical pollutants released into the atmosphere, the soil, the rivers and the oceans - it is a tribute to the resilience of planet earth, that energy renewal still takes place.

The Earth cleanses itself

The Earth cleanses itself by cyclonic activity. The increased disruption of the weather, that is popularly and loosely ascribed to global warming, is a natural effect of the planetary weather purifying the atmosphere. Though such storms as hurricanes and tornados cause much damage, it is notable

---

[17] See also Chapter 7, the final chapter for a discussion of the Oranur experiments.

that after the storm the atmosphere once again becomes pristine. However such is the continual onslaught from chemical and radiation pollution that fresh severe cyclonic activity soon manifests again. It is doubly unfortunate that the areas most damaged by such destructive weather are seldom the areas that create the most pollution. The purification that occurs from storms follows the laws of weather functioning, of which we are still profoundly ignorant.

The weather is also interplanetary. Though man-made pollution profoundly affects weather, there is a cosmic influence of which we also know little. We must keep in mind that the Sun also has 'weather' as manifested by solar flares and sunspots[18]. But there is a relationship between sunspot activity and the Earth's weather. There is some correlation that indicates drier and warmer weather on Earth during times of sunspot maximum and wetter colder weather during sunspot minimum. This is an aspect of 'weather', which is not only interplanetary, but reflects the metabolism of the local star cluster in which the solar system is embedded.

The importance of the concept of Cosmic Metabolism

To recapitulate; the concept of Cosmic Metabolism; the turning point, the missing cosmological link, that underpins the concept, is that of transformation. When entropic energy reaches maximum expansion, it transforms into condensative energy, the formative energy of the universe. No longer expansive, it is renewed by space and then begins its condensative cycle, eventually forming new matter. It is starlight, in fact the entire spectrum of stellar energy, that condenses through the medium of the terrestrial vortex into new matter, the prime constituents of which are Hydrogen, Oxygen, Nitrogen and Carbon - the prime constituents of both the atmosphere and of life itself. These are transformations that involve the actual creation of matter. Scientists have failed to realise this, because of an a priori belief that the only possible elemental transformations are those involving nuclear physics.

It is notable that such transformations brought about through nuclear physics, are mostly unstable and decay into atomic structures lower in the periodic table. But of course one would not expect otherwise - as nuclear physics belong to the entropic aspect of the cosmic duality. In naturally occurring cosmic metabolism, the expansive energy reaches ultimate expansion unimpeded by containing devices, such as internal combustion engines or turbines. For the dissipative energy to be renewed, Space is necessary. It is the function of cleaning waste energy. Space is functionally opposite to matter - as is perhaps obvious - but is significant in a much more profound sense than is generally realised.

This revolutionary view resolves many of the inconsistencies of orthodox cosmology. As pointed out orthodoxy accepts the concept of relativity, yet still postulates an absolute origin. Orthodoxy views entropy, not as a

---

[18] Sunspots are cyclonic activity at the Sun's surface

function but as an end process. Thus it considers entropic energy "lost" once it has dissipated beyond the point where it is useful to mankind. If this were the ultimate truth, space would have long ago become filled with stagnant energy from dissipating stellar radiation. And it is from this pessimistic misunderstanding that the concept of the cosmic "heat death" is derived.

Atmospheric energy

However there is a grain of truth in the concept of "heat death" at least in a local sense. On earth today so much secondary entropic energy is released from factories, automobiles, aircraft, nuclear reactors etc, that this frequently exceeds the atmosphere's ability to metabolise and transform pollution. We experience palls of stagnant energy especially over cities. Such occurrences are blamed on "temperature inversions". A layer of cold air rests over a blanket of polluted air, which remains trapped, resulting in even more pollution. Science has given no feasible explanation as to how this situation can arise. But it is similar to what occurred when Reich initiated the Oranur experimentation. The atmospheric energy that normally provides us with fresh air, turns into a killer energy, under which all life stagnates. The conditions can persist for weeks, until like a sick organism overthrowing a disease, a weather crisis develops, usually some kind of storm condition and only then the pollution clears. Unfortunately the period of clean atmosphere seldom lasts long as the pollutants soon build up again and the cycle recommences.

Faced with this problem as a result of placing small amounts of radioactive material within Orgone accumulating devices, Reich's discovery that a number of copper tubes assembled in parallel and connected to a large water source (in his case a large lake) will initiate an atmospheric drawing action, eventually dispersing the stagnant energy, have still been ignored.

Section 4

Conclusions – Not just the carbon footprint but crucially the radiation footprint

The relevance of Reich's later research to current environmental debates

Chapter 6. Science is tied up in packages
The energy potential we ignore

"Today's scientists have substituted mathematics for experiments and then have wandered off through equation after equation and eventually build a structure which has no relation to reality."

Nikola Tesla

Engaging scientists in debates

I am sure you now have an idea about cosmic energy and Cosmic Metabolism. So why do scientists not yet accept such a concept of cosmic energy? I believe it is because of the challenge it poses and how the scientific world deals with that. This has important implications for the scientific world's capacity to look openly at the current environmental crisis and provide us with possible solutions.

In the 1940's, as a teenager, I was not in a position to challenge astronomical ideas, even if they seemed to be contradicted by what I saw. I was just learning about what had been found and what opinions were.

In the 1950's in New York in my twenties it was not a question of looking for something challenging, I was initially focused on jazz but I had already become involved in a study of psychology. I discussed Freud and Reich as I have said with Lennie Tristano and other jazz musicians.

By the 1960's I had been reading, studying, researching and experimenting sufficiently to realise a new validity. As I explained in Chapter 3, it is one thing to understand a new concept and another thing to try and write about it, especially when it contradicts so much of what people have come to believe. But then it is another thing to write about it and then try for many years to engage with scientists (and academics) about it.

Reaction in Big Sur

It was not until 1963 when I went to Big Sur, California and I was really trying to set down what I had learnt in "Cosmic Metabolism and Vortical Accretion" that I began to talk about this with people in that community, including some scientists and academics. Initially the reaction seemed positive.

I had asked the people who attended my Esalen lecture if they were interested in contributing to the cost of printing my writing as a book. Their contribution would ensure that they got a copy of the book once it was published. I think I asked them to contribute $15. Many did and perhaps this gave me a false hope about sharing these concepts.

But they were people that I would have seen as a good cross section of opinion. For example, William Chenery, who had been the head of Collier's publishing, had attended the lecture. I used to do work clearing scrub etc on his estate once a week (jazz musicians continually need to make ends meet). When I finally got the book printed I gave him a copy and some time later he came and shook my hand and said, " I have read your book. It is impressive and it is an honour to know you" in those words. Comforting words from a retired executive to his handyman!

I had met Wayne Nowack, the artist and his wife Jean earlier and we suggested they came to Big Sur, which they did after a stay in Mexico. At that time he was a lecturer in art on sabbatical from a New York college. We had discussed the content of the book many times before I published it and for him it was the affirmation of what we had talked about. Up until his death in 2004 we had a long and continuous correspondence about Cosmic Metabolism, which he supported.

Giles Healey and his wife Sheila were another couple living in Big Sur, whom I met and had discussions with and who attended the lecture. He was a geodesist, who had retired but was called out of retirement periodically by the US government as an expert on global positioning at the beginning of satellite technology. He too was very supportive. In fact he likened me to Grote Reber, who was the first man to detect radio emissions from both the sun and the Milky Way and had built a thirty-foot dish in his backyard in Illinois. This was actually the first radio telescope. Imagine being his neighbour in the nineteen thirties with a dish of roof height next door!

There were many others who came to the lecture and showed interest even if they did not comment on the book in detail, including Lyon Phelps, who was a poet and a scion of the Phelps family, the founders of Harvard University and Mary Crile, who was the widow of George Crile, a well-known doctor of alternative medicine. Radio Astronomer Allan Seeger (the brother of Pete Seeger the American folk singer and songwriter) came specifically to see me in Big Sur, after the book's publication and was positive about the concept of Cosmic Metabolism. So within the Big Sur community there was a significant number of academics, scientists and wealthy business people who seemed to be supportive. I did not then have a sense that these ideas were unacceptable. Maybe, as I am sure some will say, it was after all California and in the sixties and what else did I expect? But maybe people at that time were more open to such concepts.

Other reactions

But I was very aware that there were contradictory opinions about Reich's work. In fact someone I see as very significant alongside Reich, Immanuel Velikovsky, was one of those. He was an academic from Princeton who wrote "Worlds in Collision" which was a big seller but very controversial at that time. I wrote to him after I had published my book and sent him a copy and he wrote back (I still have the letter) and said that I seemed sincere but that he had no regard for what he called the "tragic Reich". In this context it is interesting that both Velikovsky and Reich had been Freud's associates. Even though Velikovsky had himself been the subject of much controversy, he was not open to Reich's work. What happened to Reich could be seen as tragic but that does not invalidate his work.

So at the time of writing I knew the 1964 book was challenging but I had no idea just how the scientific community would subsequently reject what I had written. I sent copies of the book in 1964 to various institutions, including the prestigious publications - Scientific American and Sky and Telescope. I received no response from the former but Sky and Telescope replied that it was unsuitable for review in their publication.

In 1964, my book had been aimed mainly at the astronomical profession. When I wrote it I had not realised how impossible it was for an outsider to influence that profession, especially in trying to introduce critical new concepts. At that time, in my early thirties, I believed (rather naively as I later saw it), that by setting out clearly what Reich had discovered and comparing it with the views of orthodox astronomy that it might lead to a re-evaluation of our understanding of outer space. It subsequently became clear that this had been a vain hope. Any further conversations I had with scientists always seemed to result in a dismissal of Reich.

Back in the UK trying to discuss Cosmic Metabolism with scientists in 1973

In 1973, a TV programme was commissioned, about me, made for Thames Television. As ever I discussed Reich's work as an integral part of my thinking about life energy and how that had influenced my playing and painting. Jeremy Isaacs, the head of Thames at that time, took out all references to Reich! Shortly after, I discovered, in a reference, that an ex-BBC journalist came across a BBC memo that forbad any reference about Reich. I cannot now verify that but would be fascinated if someone else could!

Part of the filming was done at Oxford Scientific Films and there was a discussion with Peter Parks the founder. There was also discussion with a Professor at Sussex University, a biologist. There were further discussions and filming at the Cranfield Institute of Technology and at Imperial College in London filming other interviews with academics there. Two things that struck me about this whole process. Firstly what was interesting was the apparent prestige of Thames TV and the respect paid to my ideas when they were discussed as part of the filming. Secondly they were all effectively dismissive of Reich and therefore of me really - even during the filming I began to be regarded as a maverick. The discussions were often uncomfortable. They were unwilling to accept any of my arguments but nevertheless seemed unable or unwilling to counter them effectively. I found it very unsatisfactory.

However, one bright outcome was that we went to the Courtauld Gallery in London. This contained some well-known paintings by Van Gogh. In the film I discussed at this location the fact that Van Gogh saw and understood the cosmic energy that he depicted so vividly in his work. What was remarkable to me, and fundamentally underlined what I was trying to show, was that under strong TV lighting the pictures appeared, as they must have done outdoors when he painted them. This gave me a stronger conviction of his portrayal of energy. For me personally that was the high spot of the film.

It was the same year that I went to the US and stayed with my ex- wife's family. Her brother was a friend of Professor Charles Whitney, professor of astronomy at Harvard University. I went to see the professor, which I discussed in Chapter 4. His conclusion was very significant; he said that maybe I had something but that no matter whether I was right or not it was not possible to counter Einstein. Unsurprisingly the meeting did not end convivially.

Nor did I have much luck with those organisations focused on an alternative perspective of science. I contacted the Science of Mind group in London. Even with this group I found it difficult to open up any serious discussion, because the people involved in this group were almost exclusively focused on their own concepts and trying to gain acceptance of them. I suppose I was too!

A changed context - 1979

Having written the 1979 essay, I sent a copy to the Reichian Institute as it was then (this was twenty two years after Reich's death), hoping to add my voice to those who supported Reich's work. As I mentioned in Chapter 3, the person who replied to it - a woman by the name of Lois Wyvell - wrote to me an irate letter claiming that it was Reich who had conceived Cosmic Metabolism and that I had plagiarised his work. However Reich had not even mentioned such a concept in any of his writings, let alone explained its significance. It just was not a part of his vision. It was as though she wanted to claim everything that followed on from Reich's work as being something that was inalienably his. I am sure, from everything that I have read, that would not have been Reich's position had he still been alive.

I can understand her concern. In the intervening time since Reich's death, there have been developed a host of therapeutic methods clearly influenced, directly or indirectly by Reich's writings. Few of these contributions or additions to Reich's work have acknowledged his influence.

This has happened many times in the scientific community. For example, Johannes Kepler is rightfully recognised as the formulator of the planetary laws of equal areas in equal times - concerning planetary movement around the sun. It is equally clear that without Tycho Brae's prior observations of apparent planetary positions as observed from the earth, that finally displaced the less accurate concepts of Ptolemy - concepts that had been accepted for the centuries since Roman times - Kepler would not have been able to deduce the remarkable fact of the planets covering equal areas in equal times in their orbital movement around the sun.

It is regrettable that acknowledgments have not been given to Reich's influence. But it does not mean that any new contributions should be attributable to Reich – any more than someone – trying to claim that Kepler's work was really that of Tycho Brae.

So, even in 1979, despite wanting to make the Concept of Cosmic Metabolism known and promoting discussion of Reich's concept of cosmic energy, I realised it was still too contentious and too early. So why has there been such a reaction or dismissal of his research till now by the scientific community when demonstrated evidence is there to see? I have come to a number of conclusions about this.

Conclusions about the reaction
Threatening scientific academic positions
Firstly, new concepts of substance inevitably upset the academic world and many theoretical positions. Previous research or even sinecures are threatened as a result. There are other historical parallels. When Copernicus finally agreed to allow his thesis to be published, pointing out that the earth revolves around the sun and not vice-versa, it was at the urging of his student Georg Joachim Rheticus. Copernicus died shortly after his thesis was published, so he personally did not suffer the persecution so often meted out to originators, but his student seems to have suffered much, having been accused of being a sexual deviant. Whether or not there was substance in such accusations, it does follow a predictable pattern of rejecting that which challenges existing concepts. Wilhelm Reich's work was no exception.

Jealousy of other scientists
Secondly, I personally think that there is much to support the view that the FDA action was prompted by the jealousy of some other psychologists and psychiatrists. Of course when such an action is set in motion, it gains a momentum of its own, leading to promotion for those who successfully prosecute such actions.

The need to destroy all of Reich's work
Thirdly, it is not just a question of his being discredited but effectively

destroyed. It is the intensity with which all of Reich's work had to be wiped out that has always amazed me. In the FDA indictment everything related to the Orgone Accumulators had to be destroyed (and I mean physically broken up and destroyed). That was the injunction. But they used the injunction to take all of Reich's books and burn them. They maintained that since all of Reich's books were published by 'The Orgone Institute Press" and carried that imprint; this was "considered labelling". It is difficult not to view such action as vindictive. And so thoroughly was Reich's work destroyed, with the book burning, his death in jail and the lies that he was a quack, that now fifty years after his death his work is scarcely known outside a small circle. Even from those who have heard of him, the usual question is - "Was he the sex man?"

Apart from these personal and political dimensions, the rejection of Reich's work highlights, for me, some contradictions within scientific thinking.

The difficulty of accepting new ideas

So, fourthly, I would highlight a contradiction within current scientific debates that undermines not only the possibility of openness to new ideas but also dismisses what does not fit existing positions. Theoretical thinking in science is based on provable facts. Facts are based on evidence and evidence is based on experimentation. However theoretical thinking becomes so welded into attitudes and positions that it is difficult for any new evidence to be accepted. Remember that statement the professor made "It is not possible to counter Einstein"? Surely, if that were so, then all evidence, which might counter Einstein, would have to be dismissed rather than considered on its merits? That would not be scientific. But it is a scientific opinion.

One often hears the phrase 'scientific opinion'; it is a contradiction in terms. If it is mere opinion it is just speculation, not science. The 'big bang' versus 'steady state' debate mentioned in Chapter 2 is a case in point. The proliferation of new findings, and in particular the incredible space photography, has, like a glossy brochure, helped to give apparent credence to what will eventually be realised as a basically faulty concept. There are reasons why the big bang theory has gained credence, but these too are based upon a wrong interpretation of what is known as the red shift. I discussed this in my first publication of CMVA and in this essay I have avoided taking a path too technical and too abstruse. Suffice it to point out that the interpretation of the seeming recession of the galaxies (known as the 'red shift') is incorrect; it is simply a function of the dispersion of radiation and not some mythical cosmic expansion!

Seeing scientific evidence only within narrow compartments

Fifthly, our culture is a culture of compartmentalisation. Everything is seen only within its own parameters. In that respect there is no true cosmic outlook. In fact as I have made clear, it seems difficult for people to think in terms of the cosmos.

In addition, these positions become set. As discussed in Chapter 3, since the advent of steam power, two centuries ago, the concept of cosmic energy has remained concerned with one of expansive heat. All current cosmological theory has founded itself on this concept. So imagine what the reaction is to something that would unpick that? Only now is there a realisation that, with oil and other fossil fuels becoming increasingly harder to access and the eventual scenario of no longer depending on these sources of energy, there is the possibility to look again at energy other than fire energy.

Not understanding that Orgone energy is an everyday reality

Sixthly, the concept of organic, cosmic energy is misunderstood and it is difficult for people to understand that it is an ever-present reality! Having read about Wilhelm Reich's work, in my book Jazz Visions, people have asked me about Orgone; they want to know more. What struck me about their questioning, was their impression that Orgone was some new magical substance that had somehow been overlooked by science. The irony of this is that even many who found Reich's work to be genuine, still seemed to conceptualise Orgone as though it was a new reality. Reich in his experimental work realised what had previously been totally overlooked, but he did not invent Orgone. I only began to grasp what he wrote about when I finally looked at the world about me as imbued not with some special substance that had been previously unknown, but as a unity of life and energy that is an everyday reality.

There is increasing acceptance about there being auras, or personal energy fields, around people. In fact it is now possible to photograph these. Anyone who has experienced the heightened awareness, through such substances as mescalin or peyote, such as the writer Aldous Huxley, have also described this reality as natural – not some mystical unreal vision. But to see this does not require chemicals or mystical enlightenment. Those who have looked in detail and just painted what they saw – the Impressionist artists at the turn of the century, just represented what they saw in terms of energy. The Impressionists, particularly Cezanne, Pissaro, and Monet – painted this reality and it brought to the world a new awareness of light and vision that most previous artists failed to realise. Another Impressionist painter, Seurat, depicted the auric aspect of the atmosphere, and though sometimes criticised as stiff in contrast to other impressionists, nevertheless conveyed another aspect of this energetic reality. The most significant artist in this respect was of course Vincent Van Gogh, who not only conveyed the reality of the energy field, but more especially its universal movement. Such pictures as The Starry Night, or the canvasses of Cypresses in a Field, convey such an overwhelming presence of energetic unity, that he rightly became heralded as one of the supreme artists of all time. The later Impressionist painters, such as Vuillard and Bonnard – although featuring mainly indoor impressions, also convey the reality of the energy fields within a room. One critic described Bonnard's work as the impression you get when you first enter a strange room before your senses have rationalised what you see. So there are those who have recognised what Reich termed Orgone energy, as part of everyday reality.

Cutting across an established outlook

Lastly, the main underlying reason why Reich's concept of Orgone has been overlooked is not that it was or is some strange new reality. It is because it cuts across an established outlook, welded within the culture we live in. In this respect much of Impressionist art has been viewed as though some unique view of reality, briefly shared by a small group of European artists. What art remains from that brief period, mainly centred in France during the latter part of the nineteenth century, is now treated merely as valuable antique art, not as contributions to our enlightenment of planetary and cosmic reality. True the atmosphere has changed considerably since those days of mainly smoke pollution. Seldom in impressionist pictures do we see the kind of skies so common today, though impressionists often depicted pollution. Monet's picture of the Gare St Lazare in Paris for example, the energy depicted is still strong. A sense of excitement and energy lies in such pictures, despite the smoke from locomotives or from factory chimneys.

Look at the contrast of today's skies, so often low grey skies of sullen black-brown clouds, with hazy edges. Consider also vegetation that flowers often before and beyond the natural season. One has to be old enough to really appreciate how the world of energy has changed, mainly to its detriment. But a tour of art galleries featuring Impressionist art can reaffirm that earlier reality, even for those too young to have experienced personally the atmospheric changes wrought since the advent of nuclear pollution. Painting landscapes today, I describe myself as a post-nuclear Impressionist painter, concerned to depict the energy all around but also reflecting the changes in the environment, particularly trees in this time of radiation pollution.

For all of the reasons above, Reich's work has been denied, criticised or ignored. Only now are there emerging signs of a resurgence of thinking about pollution with the need to reconsider alternative sources of energy to fossil fuel. It is therefore particularly important that we have the confidence to ask questions and make sure that we are not being persuaded by others because they position themselves as the authority on pollution and environmental solutions, rather than because they have the knowledge. For example, I hear so many dire warnings about global warming. Although there is increasing evidence of climate change, the concept of global warming is not born out by the research. It appears that, since the industrial revolution over two centuries ago, the temperature of the Earth has increased only .7 degrees Celsius - a very minor amount compared to the dire warnings we see in the media.

Perhaps there will be a new generation of environmentalists, if not scientists, open to the concepts Reich has brought into the world and able to see the relevance of these to our future.

Chapter 7 – Reflecting again on Reich in 2007
Thinking about the Earth

"If I have seen further it is by standing on the shoulders of giants."
Isaac Newton

Reich's later research

So far in this essay I have outlined why I think Reich's work is so important. I discussed briefly what his work meant to me. I have also tried to explain, in more technical details in Section 2 and 3 what I think his research and experiments proved. To draw this essay to a close I want to summarise the key points and reflect on the continuing relevance of his research to debates about pollution and the environment.

Wilhelm Reich held a deserved place in psychology – especially for his concepts of the principles of character analysis. His later research and breakthrough into Orgone therapy – with his elucidation of the specific life energy – resulted in many of his former followers, being unable or unwilling thereafter to follow his concepts or acknowledge his research. This of course raises the question as to why?

At the start of this essay I did not, on purpose, explain in any detail the nature of the case brought against him. I thought it necessary to present his discoveries first without entering into a long dialogue about what led to the injunction and why he was jailed. I did not want to prejudice the reader – especially those who still might believe that the state is omnipotent and would not resort to such drastic measures as an injunction without good reason against someone who already had an international reputation.

To look now at what led to the claim that Reich was in effect a fraud or a charlatan lies in his later research. The FDA claimed that Orgone energy does not exist and, on those grounds, all of those concepts of Orgone energy were deemed fraudulent and the Orgone Accumulators completely destroyed. The FDA never proved their assertions. In fact, Reich was not jailed for this in the end but for contempt of court. The original trial date was changed. In the meantime he was working and experimenting in Arizona and, according to those close to him, he did not receive notification of the change. In fact he had, in the meantime, written to the original judge claiming that the courts did not have the power to judge scientific work; that it was not within the domain of the courts. This was in response to the injunction.

I believe that most of those who lost confidence in Reich's later work did not understand its relevance as an integral part of his life work. In fact he is often referred to as having become schizophrenic; that his work up until the later research is still of relevance but that somehow he went off the rails, lost the plot or simply lost it. But I see an amount of inconsistency in these kinds of opinions.

Firstly his experiments are clearly set out for people to see. The research is there and if one believes in the scientific method, then the only way forward is by verifying the experimentation. It is not a matter of mere opinion. How many of those who gave up on Reich actually took the step of repeating his experiments? I wonder how many people formulate an opinion, for or against, without carrying out or being witness to the experimentation?

Secondly, there is no reason not to verify Reich's experiments. Generally experimentation is costly. Also in our culture, we have amassed considerable knowledge as a result of detailed and painstaking experimentation. We do not need to know as individuals the mechanisms that function in an automobile. Practical knowledge of how to operate such a machine are all that is needed (except of course if a breakdown occurs.) The cultural reality is that an automobile has a long history of success. We naturally take this for granted when we set off on our journey. However where there is doubt or a radical proposal then, unless one has faith in the potential outcome, experimentation is needed to verify what the results will be. But research can be a costly business and these days difficult to find funding support unless the funding body has the faith or confidence that funding would be merited. One only needs to consider the frustration experienced by Frank Whittle, trying to get sufficient backing to produce a working jet engine, to understand such difficulties.

However, this is not the case with Reich's experiments and research into life energy. Little capital outlay is needed. It then boils down to time and patience. So why have more people not taken a scientific perspective about Reich's research? Perhaps Reich himself has one answer. He pointed out, that in a severely armoured individual, one in whom genitality is felt as a threat, the ability to carry out orgone research is necessarily compromised.

The relevance of Reich's work to global pollution

Unlike the times when Reich was alive, there is now considerable awareness and concern, that humanity is faced with a crisis of global pollution and potential shortages of fossil fuels to enable us to continue in the way we have been accustomed.

The irony, for me, is that it was precisely Reich's own research that pointed the way forward. Yet a government seemingly intent upon its curtailment destroyed that very research. You need to go through the proof yourself to see if this was a fair democratic trial. To me there are some unexplained issues about the whole process. I was clearly told to mind my own business when, in 1954, I visited the Manhattan offices of the US Food and Drug

Administration. There always seemed to be such a total denial of Reich. It seems so strange to me.

To recap, Reich's research showed that our own idea of energy only covers one aspect of energy. Though the concept of energy obtained through combustion is known and has long been accepted, our present culture denies the reality of a fundamental cosmic energy. Neither does it understand that cosmic energy manifests as life energy, even though this has been identified in different cultures, as in Chinese and Indian concepts of medicine and health. I pointed out at the start of this essay that our culture uses electricity under the fundamental misconception that electricity is merely a displacement of electrons within a circuit. It fails to even conceptualise (let alone understand) that electricity is the fundamental cosmic energy that has been coerced (through magnetic vortices) into a form of usable energy that we exploit without an inkling of its true reality.

Since the time of the development of the steam engine, two centuries ago, humanity has built an incredible technological civilisation that seemingly has transcended every former culture. Yet now at its very summit, we find ourselves concerned that not only are we poisoning ourselves and our environment, but we are beginning to face the coming scarcity of fossil fuel resources that we have so thoughtlessly squandered. The reality is that now, we desperately need a solution, a solution that ironically Reich understood in essence, yet his insight was discarded as fraudulent!

Looking Again at Global Warming

Against this background let us look at the current views on how to deal with this apparently insuperable task of what is sometimes viewed as global warming, and at others as climate change. It has become clear that human activities have had an effect not only upon the global weather, but also on vegetation, the well-being of the oceans, the polar ice caps and possibly also affecting plate tectonics.

Two basic points need to be kept in mind. 1/ Weather has always been unpredictable - even before the massive interference of the last half century. 2/ As scientists are now beginning to realise, we are not just a planet isolated in empty space but are part of a cosmic weather system of which as yet we know little.

Following my own work in reaffirming the reality of Reich's discoveries I realised the principle of what I termed Cosmic Metabolism as the process of energy renewal. To reiterate, Space is not a functionless void but an essential counterpart to material bodies that inhabit space. The essence of space is purification - the energy emitted from material bodies - diffuses into space where it eventually becomes renewed. Space is the medium through which that renewal or cleansing takes place. Unlike the Newtonian view of empty space inhabited by bodies held together by gravitation, and regulated by clockwork, space has a function akin to the living. There is a constant process of renewal - essentially a process in which tired energy dissipates and in expanding into deep space is renewed, finally condensing once more in to living energy and matter. It even happens locally on earth.

Our processes of sewage treatment embody the same principle, albeit on a limited scale. That we have not been aware of the profound significance of such processes is due to our own limitations of cosmic awareness. We know how to treat sewage from experience. It is another matter to recognise and understand why such processes as flotation and re-oxygenation work.

It is not enough just to accept that a process works, as though unrelated to anything of deeper significance! We need to look at such processes within a wider context. It might at first seem too big to grasp. It might seem frightening or unrelated to our everyday lives but it is crucial to see the link of the cosmos to our own existence.

Our civilisation is reaching a position where the natural metabolic processes are insufficient to maintain a healthy atmosphere or to maintain healthy oceans and land. The effect on all living things is apparent. Fishes in lakes and in the oceans suffer and die, trees and other vegetation becomes diseased and dies. In trying to mitigate such problems we use pesticides, and all manner of chemical remedies, that although superficially advantageous, only exacerbate the problem in the long run. As humans we rely more and more upon medicine to alleviate problems that stem largely from living on a poisoned planet. Do I paint an unnecessarily gloomy picture? Maybe so but I am hopeful that, if we understand clearly how we are affecting the capacity of Earth to cleanse itself, then there is hope for the future.

The Carbon Footprint

Recently there has been considerable attention to what has been described as the "carbon footprint". This is an abbreviation encompassing all of the processes that increase the amount of carbon released into the atmosphere, the land or the oceans. Almost without exception this concerns combustion. In taking combustible material of whatever form and igniting it – whether for motive power such as flight or other transport; whether fired to produce electricity, or simply for heating, we also need to be aware that it is not merely the increase of carbon released into the environment that is of concern, but perhaps even more importantly the consumption of oxygen without which burning could not take place.

There is often a tendency to focus on one element of the problem as though to take our minds away from the complexity of the difficulties we face. "Oh once we organise our carbon footprint by trading our pollution with that of less polluting countries the problem will be resolved" – so goes the argument. However the atmosphere does not recognise such emission trading polemics.

By using the catchphrase 'carbon footprint' we tend to avoid the more serious aspect of the reduction in available atmospheric oxygen. As we know from sewage treatment, oxygen plays a pivotal role in transforming sewage waste. It is of course essential for all except certain primitive forms of life such as anaerobic bacteria. Vast areas of the oceans are now suffering from oxygen starvation, and we are just realising that this is one of the prime symptoms of fish disease and ocean desertification.

It is not merely a problem of reducing the amount of carbon consumed, whether of fossil fuels or combustion of plant matter, the fact that oxygen reduction is perhaps of even more importance is overlooked. It is not just seriously ill hospital patients that need oxygen. We all do and as time goes by the amount of atmospheric oxygen available to us is decreasing.

There are other aspects of the atmosphere that we need to be aware of. One of the less noted aspects of weather is that on occasion, without apparent cause, the weather will suddenly clear and we experience a day or so of old fashioned pristine weather. I am sure many of us have observed such a clearing of weather following a severe storm. It is logical that the function of the storm is to clear the pollution and the tension prior to its erupting. Many people sense a build up of tension prior to a storm. One can feel this coming! Upon what senses do we rely that enable us to feel the coming storm? But what about the sudden unpredicted changes that occur almost without warning, when after a period of heavy pollution – it suddenly gives way and we feel the relief of good weather again? By good weather I do necessarily believe that this means sunshine. It can be raining, but not the kind of rain that is black with pollution. There can be the kind of gentle life giving rain that we sometimes experience in spring. We sense relief even though we may not understand what had taken place. Such realities make sense if we stop to realise that weather is not merely a local phenomenon restricted to the atmosphere, but does interact with a greater reality that scientists are only just beginning to recognise – that of space weather. We have long known the effects of solar storms and what we call sunspots and solar flares, and that earth weather is profoundly influenced by such events. But outer space weather is seldom sufficient to metabolise the growing amount of pollutants that we constantly manufacture and release. An occasional jolt from outer space weather can have a positive effect, but we need to find a solution to our own problems, not just relying on the occasional boost from interaction with cosmic weather.

Though as I pointed out earlier I do not condemn efforts to alleviate the problems of pollution that we face, I have little faith that such efforts to produce electricity through wind or waterpower will provide a genuine solution. Just supposing that by some miracle, say we have a combination of an increase of wind farms, tidal generating plants, hydroelectric facilities and an increase of nuclear facilities generating electrical power. Could this, coupled with a transport revolution using electricity, lead to an amelioration of the amount of the so-called carbon footprint?

Would this lead to a reversal of the current trend? Would we begin to experience a let up of the polluted weather that has become the planetary norm? If the cause of today's weather crisis were simply that of the carbon footprint, such a change might be possible. But underlying all of this is another factor that hardly receives any mention. This is what I might describe as the 'Radiation Footprint'. Such a concept has only just surfaced and the term is used only in relation to the mobile phone network, but it is crucial to our understanding and does not apply merely to the cell phone network but to all electronic and radio emission!

The Importance of Reich's Oranur experiments

While many people remained convinced of the validity of Reich's earlier researches, I am particularly concerned with his later Oranur – Orgone against Nuclear Energy – experiments. It is precisely those later researches and the outcome of these that led to the realisation of how to overcome the global disruption we have found ourselves in. His discovery of how weather can be influenced by the use of the "cloudbuster" is startling enough in itself, but the most important clue to understanding the dilemma of pollution, lies not simply in the cloudbusting device, but in the series of experiments that led to the development of the cloudbuster. It was this series of Oranur experiments that although witnessed by few, were the most critical aspects of his research.

During the time of the Korean War, Reich, like many scientists, was concerned with the risk of nuclear warfare. With his knowledge of the possible beneficial effects of orgone energy treatment he set out to try to find a cure for radiation sickness. It was that consideration that led to the most amazing and unanticipated series of events that were only partially resolved by the invention of the cloudbuster. Although to most people unfamiliar with orgone research, the entire process sounds like science fiction, the events themselves (though dangerous and unpredicted) were the outcome of cosmic principles that were simple in essence. It is not as though he or any of us for that matter were unfamiliar with nuclear radiation. The peculiar dangers of radiation had long been known. What was new about the Oranur research was the magnitude of the effects from minute amounts of radioactive material, beyond Reich's or any one else's anticipation. This only became apparent as he was working in an atmosphere that was heavily charged with Orgone energy.

Orthodox science regards radioactivity as phenomena peculiar to the disintegration of nuclear material. Orthodoxy, remaining unaware of the reality of the life energy, regards nuclear radiation, not as a reaction by the earth's Orgone envelope, but conceives it simply as an unrelated effect of radiating material. Current monitoring of such radiation simply views this as normal. Thus the orthodox scientific world remains unaware even today of the existence of the prime cosmic energy. Whenever it comes across such phenomena it explains it away in accordance with current mechanistic concepts.

The world at large, unaware of the reality of the cosmic energy Orgone, were of course equally unaware of Reich's discoveries and his arrangement of materials that created concentrations of that energy. His work could have been top secret as far as the rest of civilisation was concerned. In fact if it had been top secret, possibly there would have been a greater chance that the results from his research could have been accepted.

The Reality of Cosmic Energy

Therefore it is not merely a matter of reinstating Reich as a genuine and serious scientist. It is much deeper than that. It is not just taking the stance of many that here was a man of genius that somehow went off the rails with all this talk about Orgone energy. The core of the problem is humanity's failure to understand and accept the reality of cosmic energy and to realise only a partial understanding of energy. I have faced criticism and disbelief for my support of Reich's researches. As though I have identified with the underdog and that this is the reason I have pursued this course.

Not at all. I have pursued it because after taking pains to find out whether or not his writings reflect the truth, I tested what he said. Through a study of his writings and undertaking some experiments led to a conviction that the wealth of experimentation he described was not a made-up scenario. Having verified what he described, I have had no other course than to hold on to what I know.

My greatest dilemma in all this is facing the problem of persuading others in regard to this! But I know what I know.

The meeting with Dr Simeon Tropp was one of those events that confirmed what I knew to be true. Simeon had been with Reich during the most crucial Oranur experiments and described those incredible times to me. It confirmed not only my understanding of what I had read about Oranur, but also confirmed my own findings and realisations. I can do no better than to quote from Reich's own words. (From the Oranur Experiment, First Report, Orgone Institute Press 1951)

" We repeated the same experiment (placing the Radium needle in the Orgone charger) from January 5-12 daily, for one hour. On Friday the 12th of January, we undertook the last experiment in this series of daily Oranur experimentation. The experimental 1mg of Radium was put into the 20 fold Orgone charger. The results of this last experiment were so severe that they deserve to be reported in great detail. Three experimental observers remained outside the laboratory within about 100 yards. We desisted from measuring with the GM survey meter this time, in order to avoid unnecessary additional exposure. A few minutes later, we could clearly see through the large windows that the atmosphere in the laboratory had become "clouded"; it was moving visibly, and shined blue to purple through the glass. As we walked up and down some hundred to two hundred and fifty feet OUTSIDE the laboratory, all three of us had the same experience, but no one at first dared to mention it. I felt severe nausea, a slight sensation of fainting, loss of equilibrium, clouding of consciousness, and had to make an effort to keep erect on my feet. I saw Dr. S. Tropp who was with me getting very pale. He had not said anything, and I had not told him how I felt. Then I asked him how he felt, whether he felt what I felt. He immediately admitted to feeling very ill and faint, with pressure in the forehead, nauseated, cramped in the stomach, and weak. Then I confirmed his experience by mentioning my own reactions. We had both hesitated to tell about it since we were so far outside the experimental hall in the fresh, clear, dry air of a late afternoon in midwinter. There upon, we interrupted the experiment and put the radium away to half a mile distance from the laboratory, within an uninhabited area of 280 acres. It was perfectly clear from what we had experienced, that the orgone energy field of the laboratory had been greatly extended and excited to a dangerous degree far outside the outer walls." (1951: 283)

Anyone who doubts the reality of Dr. Reich's discoveries should read the "Oranur Report" and also study his further researches dealing with desert development. From this Oranur experimentation it became apparent that the atmosphere surrounding their research area had also become severely disturbed. Clouds that in the distance had been normal fluffy cumuli, upon approaching the vicinity of Orgonon, began to change, losing their shape and becoming brownish in colour, losing their cohesiveness and then becoming stuck right above the vicinity of their experimental area. It became clear that this type of weather disturbance was a direct result of Oranur experimentation. Over the years those type of clouds (Reich referred to them as DOR (Deadly Orgone clouds) have become the norm for our planet. As these changes have occurred gradually over many years, their presence seems to be taken for granted, and few today are aware of the massive atmospheric changes that have occurred during the past half-century.

The Radiation Footprint

Today we see this simply as pollution. There is no doubt regarding pollution, but what was so revealing about the Oranur experimentation was that NO CHEMICAL POLLUTION WAS INVOLVED. Chemical pollution is always blamed. But disturbance of the atmosphere through radiation paralyses the normal metabolic function of the atmosphere. This results in huge accumulations of chemical pollution around the globe, that otherwise would be metabolised normally. Failure to understand the role of radiation in interfering with normal atmospheric metabolism, points to the fact that it is not simply a matter of ceasing to create chemical pollution. The underlying problem is also one of radiation/ nuclear pollution. Thus we have to take account not only of the so called "carbon footprint", but even more importantly "the radiation or nuclear footprint". I would suggest to those avidly concerned about pollution that they consider campaigning for an equivalent way of measuring the amounts of nuclear emissions, not just from nuclear plants, but also the atmosphere generally.

And it was Reich who pointed out this radiation impact on the normal metabolic process in the atmosphere. Is that why he is so discounted? Are we talking here about another inconvenient truth? In regard to Reich, it is not simply a matter of trying to reinstate his honour as a scientist. What is essential, for our own survival on this planet, is to learn to understand the significance of all his researches.

Partial acceptance of Reich's research is tantamount to non-acceptance. To take that position merely confirms a lack of understanding that what he brought to the world transcended the parameters of existing science. Clearly his research is for the future – whether the near future, or centuries hence, rests with, as he put it, the children of the future.

It is up to all of us, to decide what we do if we understand and are open to what Reich was saying. I remain hopeful.

**Peter Ind
2007**

BIBLIOGRAPHY
Some initial references

The Function of the Orgasm (Vol 1)
Vol 2 – The Cancer Biopathy
Listen Little Man
Ether, God and Devil
Cosmic Superimposition
The Oranur Experiment – first report
Character Analysis
The Murder of Christ
The Mass Psychology of Fascism
The Sexual Revolution
Contact with Space

All by Wilhelm Reich and Published by the Orgone Institute Press

Other books by Reich
American Odyssey *Farrar Strauss and Giroux*
The Invasion of Compulsory Sex-morality *Noonday Press*
Selected Writings *Vision Press*
Reich speaks of Freud *Souvenir Press*

Books about Reich
Wilhelm Reich and Orgonomy *Ola Raknes* (St. Martin's Press)
Reich – a personal biography *Ilse Ollendorff Reich* (St.Martin's Press)
The Man who Dreamed of Tomorrow *Mann and Hoffman*
(J.P.Tarcher Inc)
The Quest for Wilhelm Reich *Colin Wilson* (Anchor Press)
Orgone, Reich and Eros *W Edward Mann* (Simon and Schuster)
Wilhelm Reich – The Evolution of his Work *David Boadella* (Dell)
WR Mysteries of the Organism *Duan Makavejev* (Bared Books (Avon))
Some Sense about Wilhelm Reich *Leo Raditsa* (Philosophical Library)
Records of a Friendship *Reich and A.S.Neill correspondence*
(Victor Gollancz)
Fury on Earth *Myron Sharaf* (Andre Deutsch)
A Book of Dreams *Peter Reich* (Harper and Row)